Eternal Sabbath

VOL. 2

Fuyumi Soryo

Translated by
Akira Tsubasa

Adapted by
Alex Kent

Lettered by
H. Jones

Ballantine Books · New York

'S, Vol. 2 is a work of fiction. Names, characters, places, and incidents are the roducts of the author's imagination or are used fictitiously. Any resemblance o actual events, locales, or persons, living or dead, is entirely coincidental.

Del Rey Trade Paperback Original

'S, Vol. 2 copyright © 2002 by Fuyumi Soryo

nglish translation copyright © 2006 by Fuyumi Soryo

ll rights reserved.

ublished in the United States by Del Rey Books, an imprint of The Random House ublishing Group, a division of Random House, Inc., New York.

EL REY is a registered trademark and the Del Rey colophon is a trademark of Random House, Inc.

ublication rights arranged through Kodansha Ltd.

irst published in Japan in 2002 by Kodansha Ltd., Tokyo.

SBN: 0-345-49189-0

Printed in the United States of America

www.delreymanga.com

9 8 7 6 5 4 3 2 1

Translator: Akira Tsubasa
Adaptor: Alex Kent
Lettering: H. Jones
Cover design: David Stevenson

Contents

Honorifics Explained

Throughout the Del Rey Manga books, you will find Japanese honorifics left intact in the translations. For those not familiar with how the Japanese use honorifics and, more important, how they differ from American honorifics, we present this brief overview.

Politeness has always been a critical facet of Japanese culture. Ever since the feudal era, when Japan was a highly stratified society, use of honorifics—which can be defined as polite speech that indicates relationship or status—has played an essential role in the Japanese language. When addressing someone in Japanese, an honorific usually takes the form of a suffix attached to one's name (example: "Asuna-san"), is used as a title at the end of one's name, or appears in place of the name itself (example: "Negi-sensei," or simply "Sensei!").

Honorifics can be expressions of respect or endearment. In the context of manga and anime, honorifics give insight into the nature of the relationship between characters. Many translations into English leave out these important honorifics and therefore distort the "feel" of the original Japanese. Because Japanese honorifics contain nuances that English honorifics lack, it is our policy at Del Rey not to translate them. Here, instead, is a guide to some of the honorifics you may encounter in Del Rey Manga.

-san: This is the most common honorific and is equivalent to Mr., Miss, Ms., or Mrs. It is the all-purpose honorific and can be used in any situation where politeness is required.

-sama: This is one level higher than "-san." It is used to confer great respect.

-dono: This comes from the word "tono," which means "lord." It is an even higher level than "-sama" and confers utmost respect.

-kun: This suffix is used at the end of boys' names to express familiarity or endearment. It is also sometimes used by men among friends, or when addressing someone younger or of a lower station.

-chan: This is used to express endearment, mostly toward girls. It is also used for little boys, pets, and even among lovers. It gives a sense of childish cuteness.

Bozu: This is an informal way to refer to a boy, similar to the English terms "kid" and "squirt."

Sempai/ Senpai: This title suggests that the addressee is one's senior in a group or organization. It is most often used in a school setting, where underclassmen refer to their upperclassmen as "sempai." It can also be used in the workplace, such as when a newer employee addresses an employee who has seniority in the company.

Kohai: This is the opposite of "sempai" and is used toward underclassmen in school or newcomers in the workplace. It connotes that the addressee is of a lower station.

Sensei: Literally meaning "one who has come before," this title is used for teachers, doctors, or masters of any profession or art.

[blank]: Usually forgotten in these lists, but perhaps the most significant difference between Japanese and English. The lack of honorific means that the speaker has permission to address the person in a very intimate way. Usually, only family, spouses, or very close friends have this kind of permission. Known as *yobisute,* it can be gratifying when someone who has earned the intimacy starts to call one by one's name without an honorific. But when that intimacy hasn't been earned, it can also be very insulting.

Isaac was raised in an artificial womb.

Because he was just a specimen to be dissected, we deprived him of stimuli to slow his mental development.
We planned to keep him there until he reached a certain age, in the dark and in silence.

His mental develop-ment...
How foolish our efforts were.

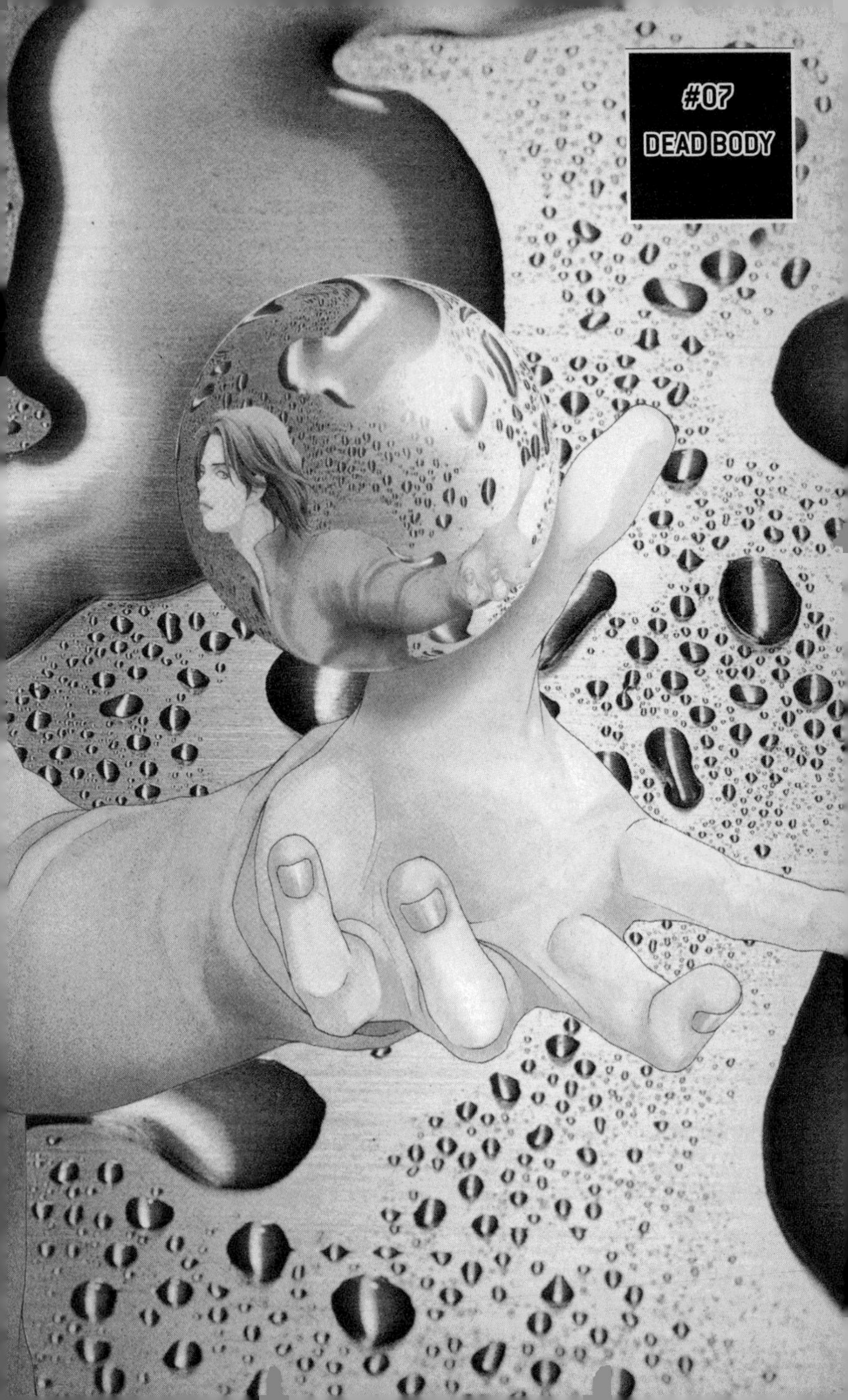
#07
DEAD BODY

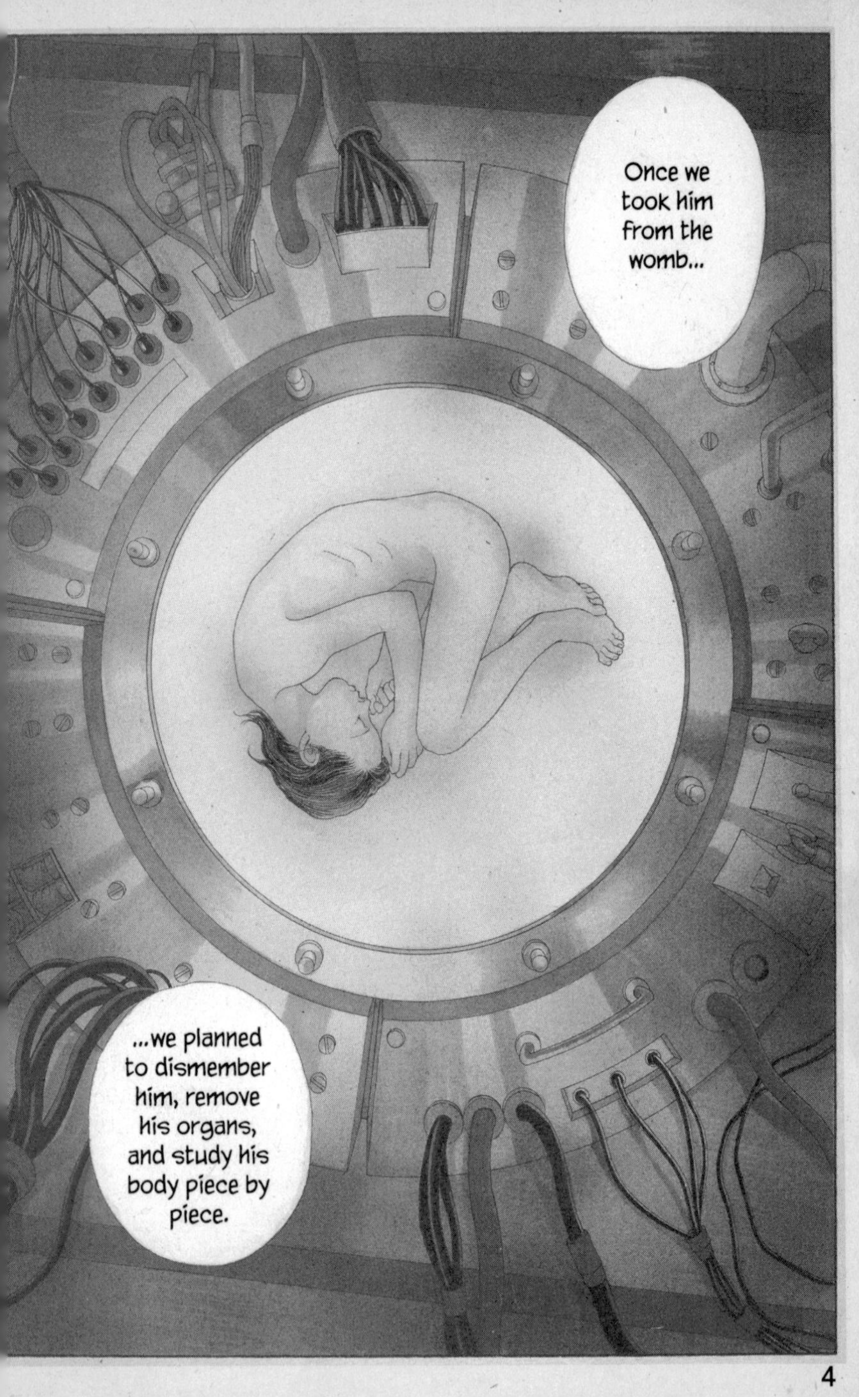
Once we took him from the womb...
...we planned to dismember him, remove his organs, and study his body piece by piece.

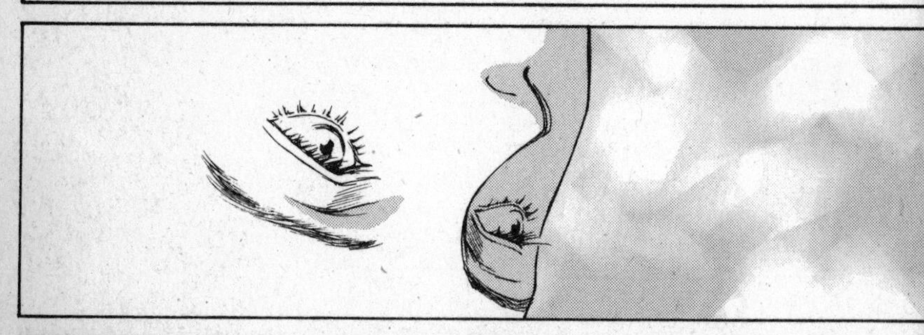

We never suspected it, but the day we released him would be our last in the lab.
It was we who were ignorant of our fate and not Isaac.

All those years in the womb, Isaac had been reading our minds.

So it was then that he attacked?

Now I can see that was just our first day in hell.
PANT はあ
PANT はあ

Actually, a month be- fore Isaac's awakening, the head re- searcher died in a strange manner.

Sakaki-san, please follow me.

Murakami-san is...

Murakami-san?

GASP

BOSU

He's dead.
But it's strange. The body is so light.

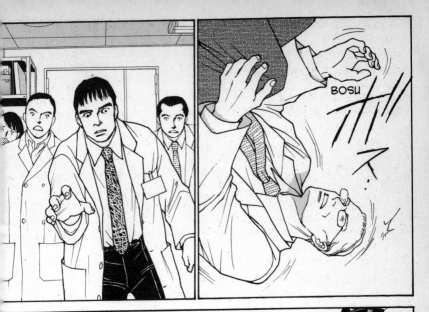

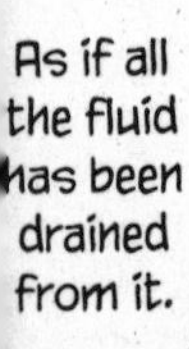
As if all the fluid has been drained from it.

Oh my God.
Just like a speci- men...

The way Murakami-san died was very unusual.
But we refused to believe that his body had really been... dehydrated.
So even after the head researcher's death, we kept on with our work.

Then one day...

KYAAAAH.

What's wrong!?
!

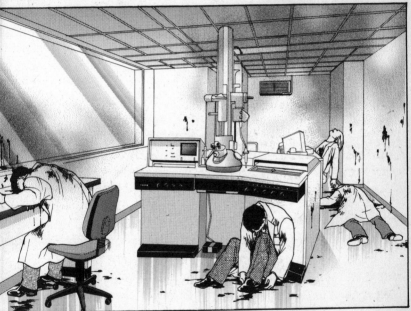

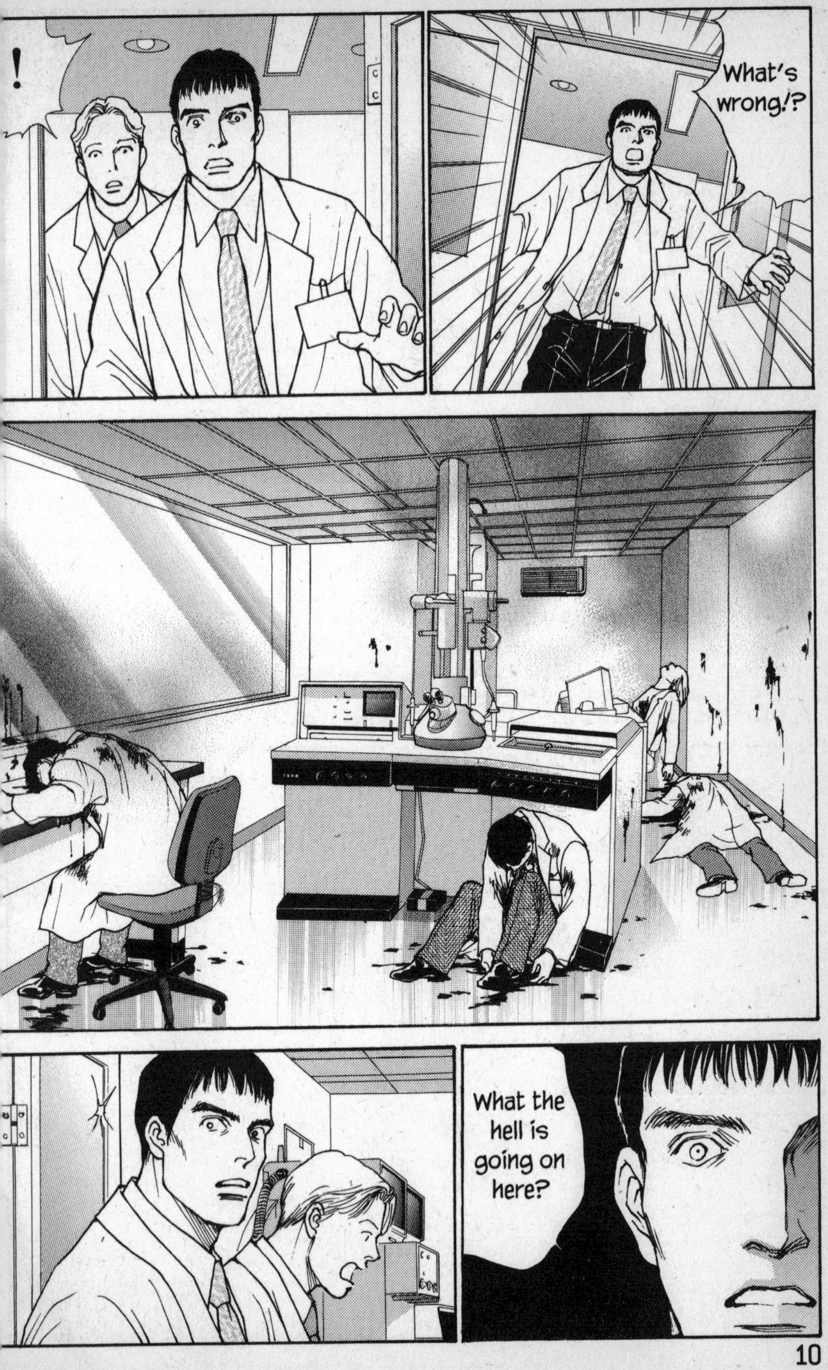

What the hell is going on here?

UWAH...
SWOOSH

UWAAAAAH.

SPLASH

UH...

URGH.
!

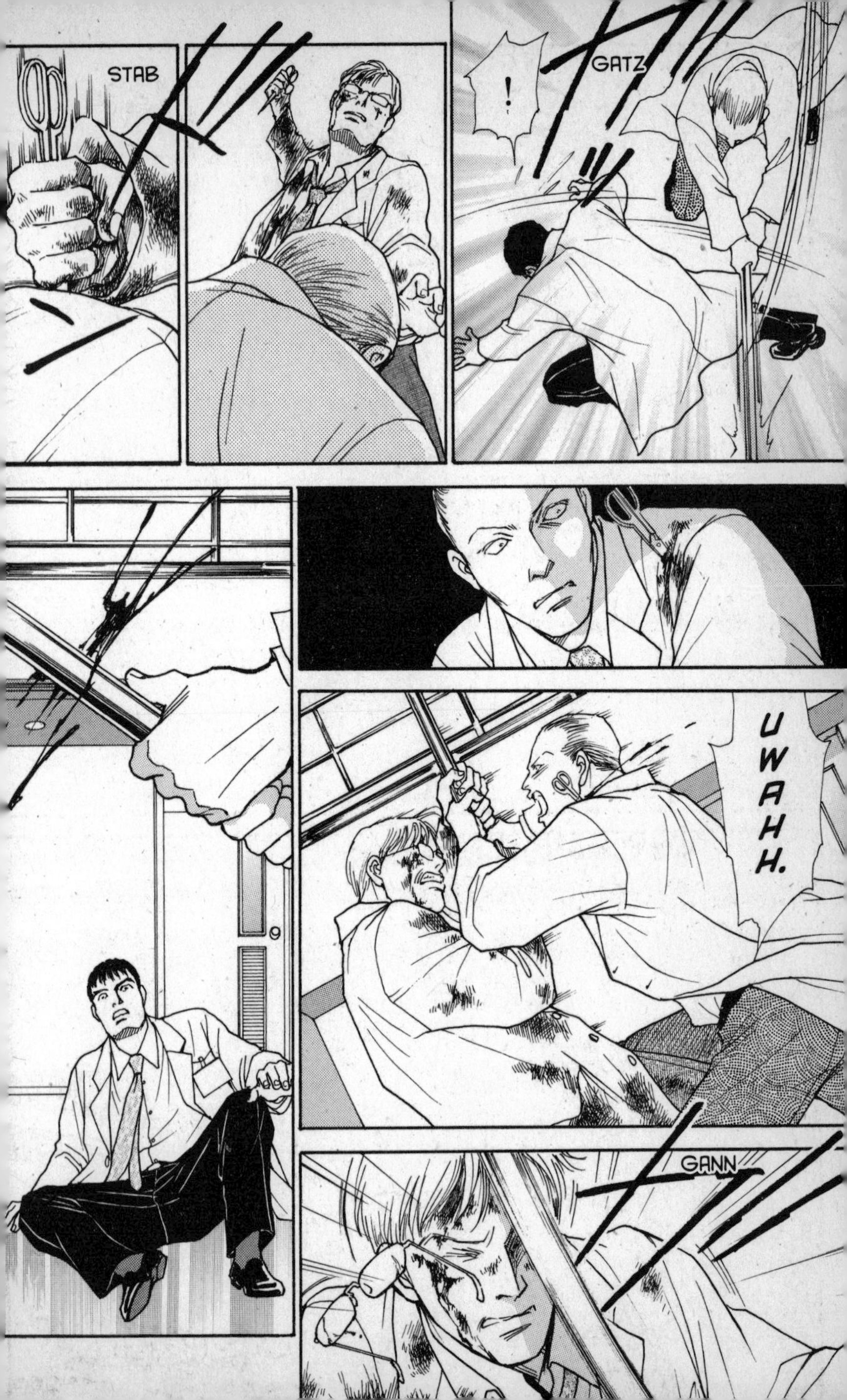
STAB
!
GATZ
UWAHH.
GANN

What the hell has hap-pened?
What's the meaning of this?
Is anybody here still sane?
They've gone mad.
They've lost their minds.

Anyone!?
Who was that?
Someone just called my name.
Over here. Please let me out.

This way.
Hurry up.

Shuro.

UWAHH!!

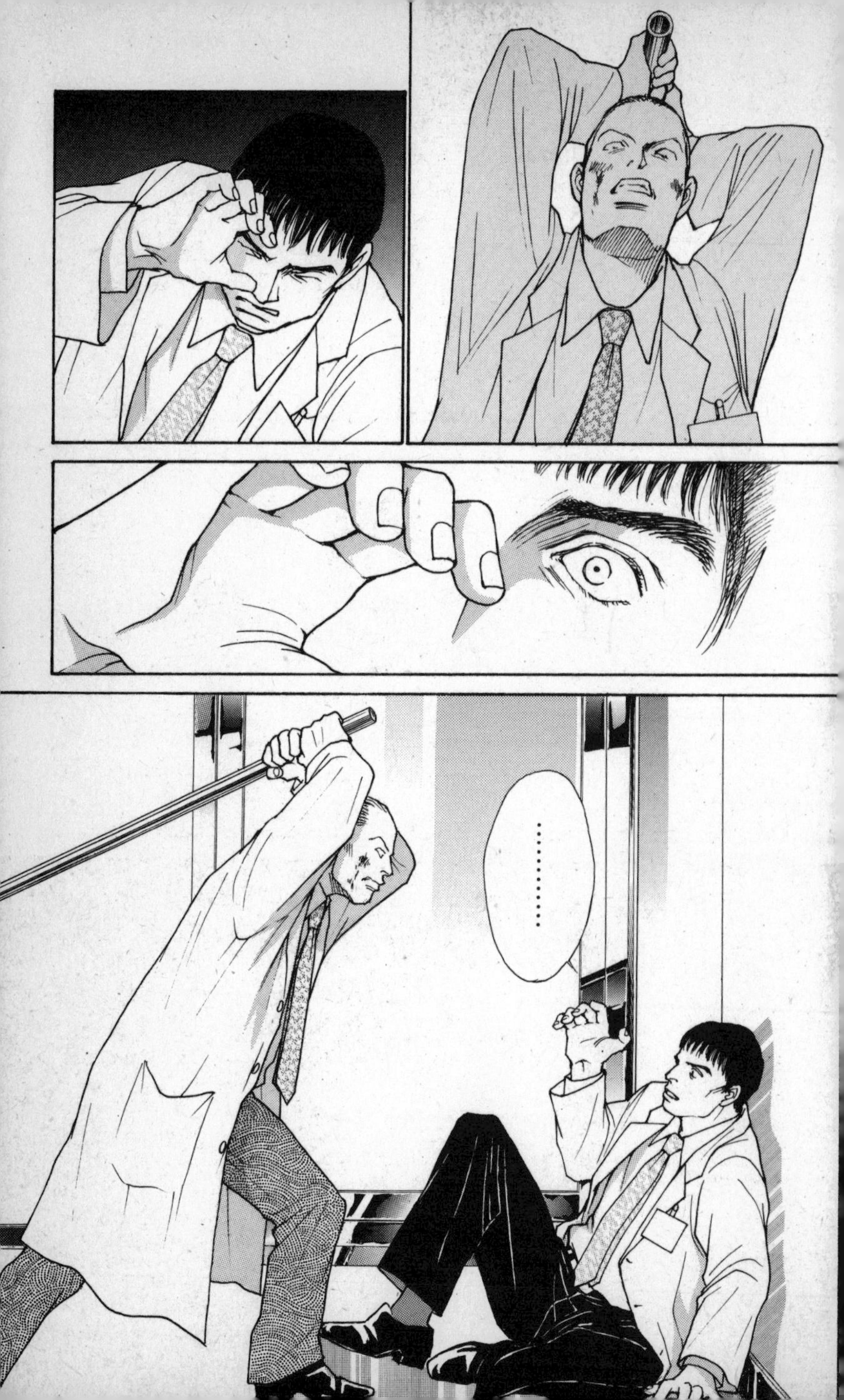

If you want to live, you have to help me.

—The end of #07 Dead Body—

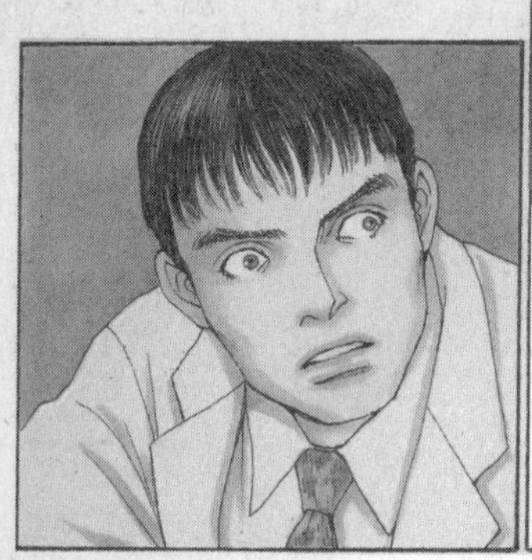

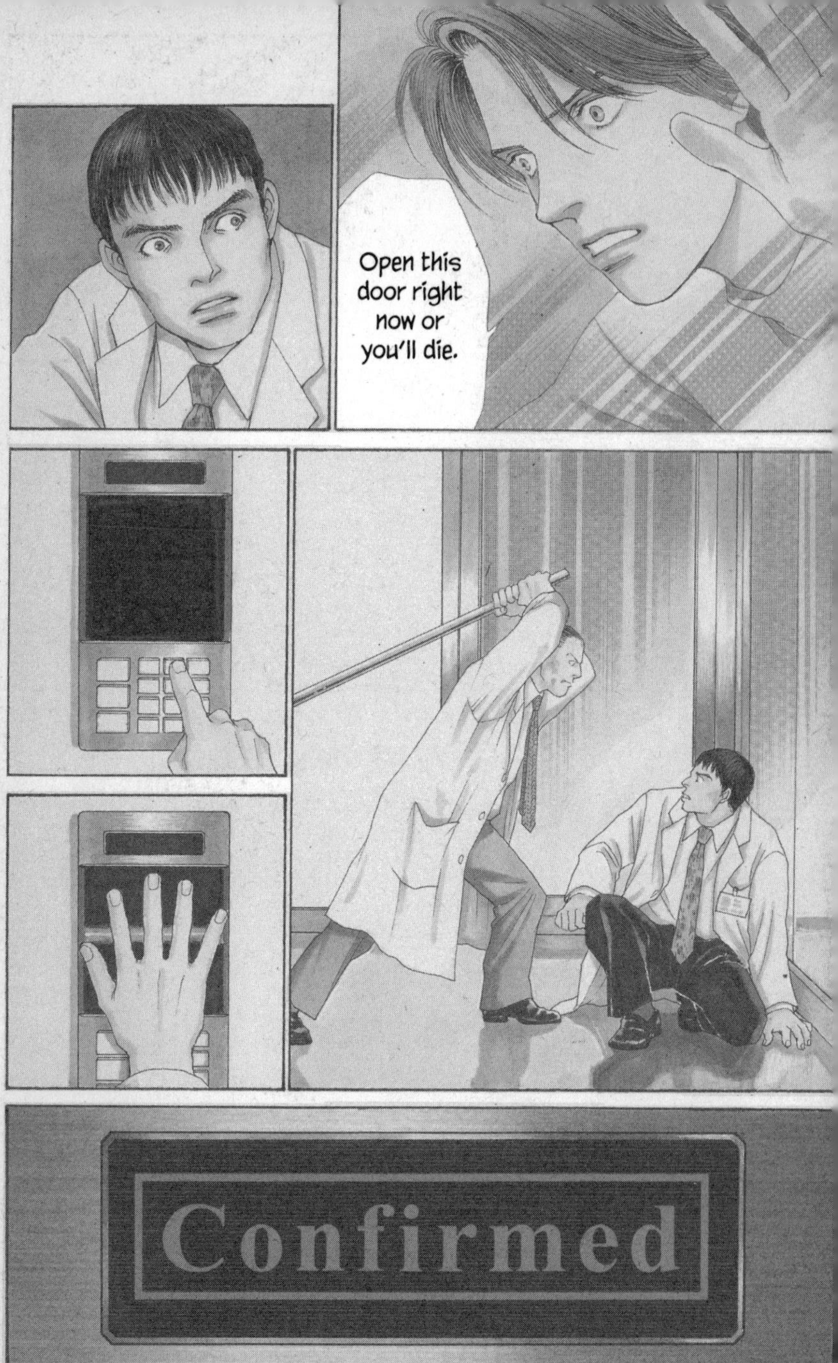

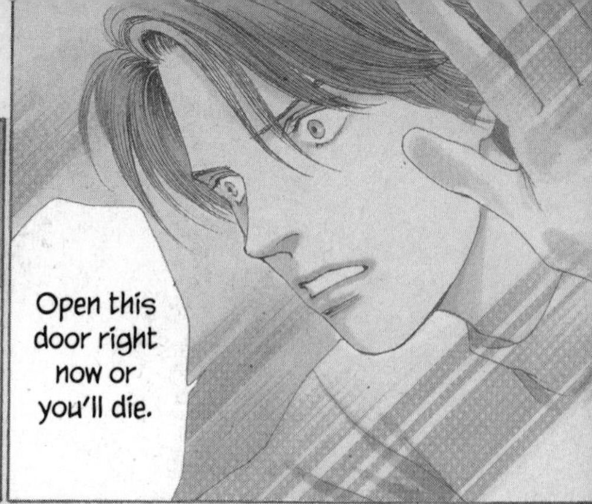

Open this door right now or you'll die.

Confirmed

#08
A SACRIFICE

I never imagined this would be the way I'd escape...

Wa... wait a minute.

Did I just see that?

What just happened to him!?

I made him stop moving.

You made him stop moving?
But how?
I went inside of his mind.
Once I entered it, I had total control of him...so I stopped him from moving.
He's even stopped breathing, so he'll die soon.
Oh, well.
We don't have time to worry about that now.
......
It's too dangerous here. We have to leave now.

You entered his mind... So the voice I heard earlier was you? Inside my mind?

Yeah. But you're hard to control, so that's pretty much all I can do to you.

I'm hard to control?

You're just not the type. There are two kinds of humans—those who are easily manipulated and those who aren't.

If you were the first kind, you would have taken part in that killing spree back there.

!

Then it was you? You created that abomination?

Please.
I have better taste than that...

The fire door's locked...

Dammit! We're trapped.

Looks like he's planning to kill us all.

Who is "he"?

DHOOON

!

What was that? It sounded like an explosion.
We have to get to the control room and find a safe escape route.
W-w-wait.
Why is Isaac doing this?
He's trying to destroy the entire building...
Because he knows...
...about your plans for him.
He found out all about it while he was trapped in that glass case.

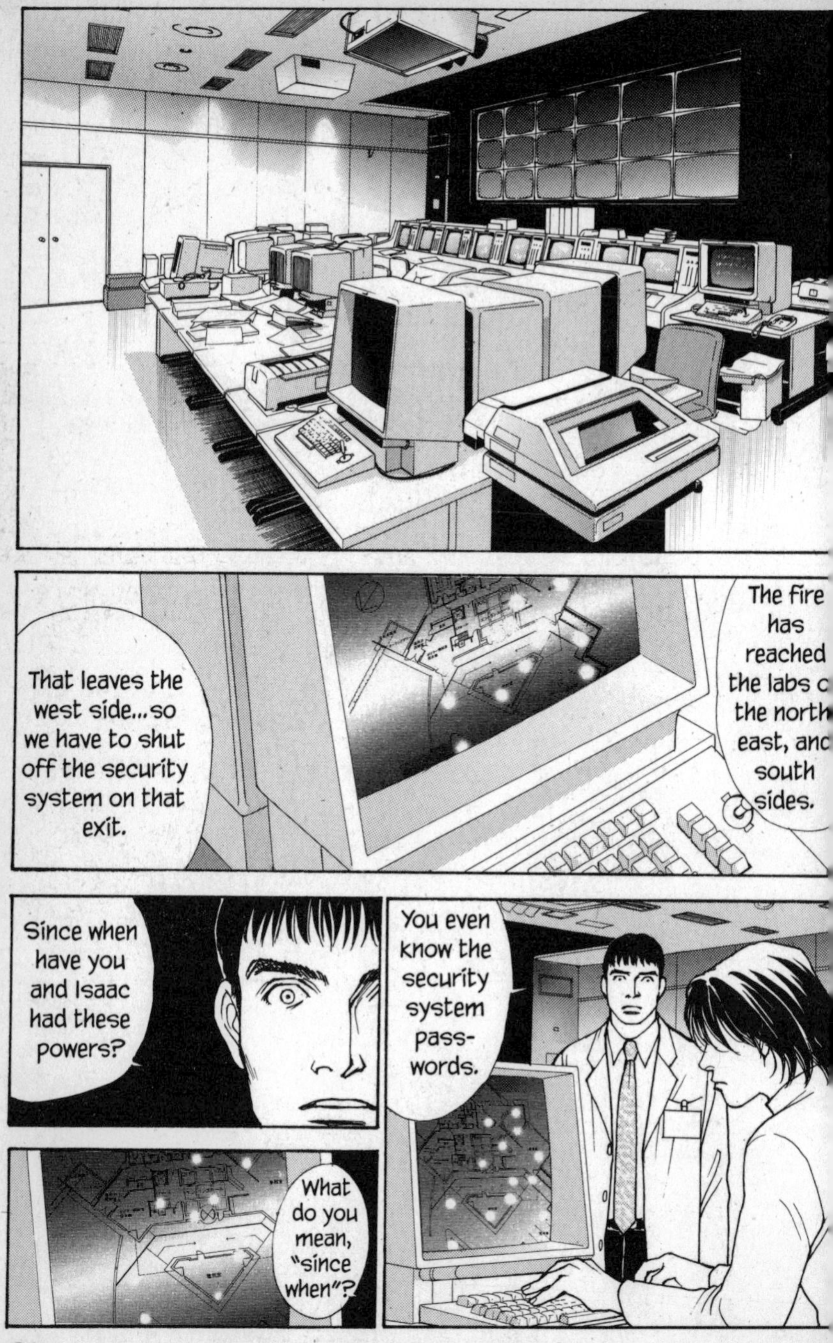

The fire has reached the labs o the north east, and south sides.

That leaves the west side...so we have to shut off the security system on that exit.

You even know the security system pass-words.

Since when have you and Isaac had these powers?

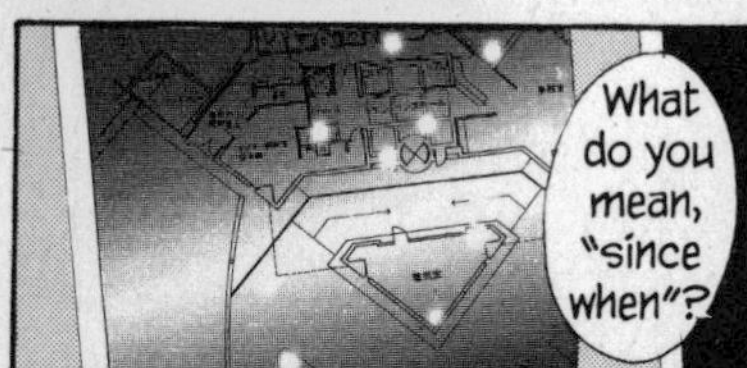

What do you mean, "since when"?

That would be since the very moment you and your buddies created us, right?

You can read minds.

But how?

Does it just happen? Or...

Be uiet. I'm trying o focus here.

KACHI

This building's pretty complex, so it's a pain in the ass to confirm the route.

KACHI

KACHI

Or maybe you can do it without me, Sakaki-san?

No...
You know more about this lab than I do.

Sweet
I turned off the alarm on the west side exit!

Let'
roll.

The fire's spreading. If we don't hurry, we'll be trapped.

Go straight to the data analysis room.

Then take a right at the end of the hall.

!

Shit.

f this is
a dream,
wake me
up now!

Hold on! I'll open the door for you.

BAM

Don't bother. Even if he escapes, Isaac will kill him.

BOWA
SNAP
SNAP
SNAP
DWOOO...N
!
GOH...

That was the last time I saw Isaac.

The lab was shut down, and so was our project.
Before I knew it, Shuro had disappeared, too.
I managed to escape, but the others weren't so lucky.

His remains weren't found in the ruins of the laboratory fire.
And I just know he's alive some-where. I can feel it.

Is Isaac really still alive?

Yes, he is.

Like Shuro, Isaac has assumed someone else's identity.

He's pretending to live a normal life.

And—

EXTENDAS • MANV • T

RVM

Trying to forget about his own miserable life

by plotting to take revenge against humankind.

The end of #08 A Sacrifice

Take revenge
I know he has unusual powers, but could a child really do such a thing?

It's possible precisely because he's a child.

#09 AN OMEN

He has the cruelty of a child who's too young to understand right and wrong.

He'll kill anyone who gets in his way.

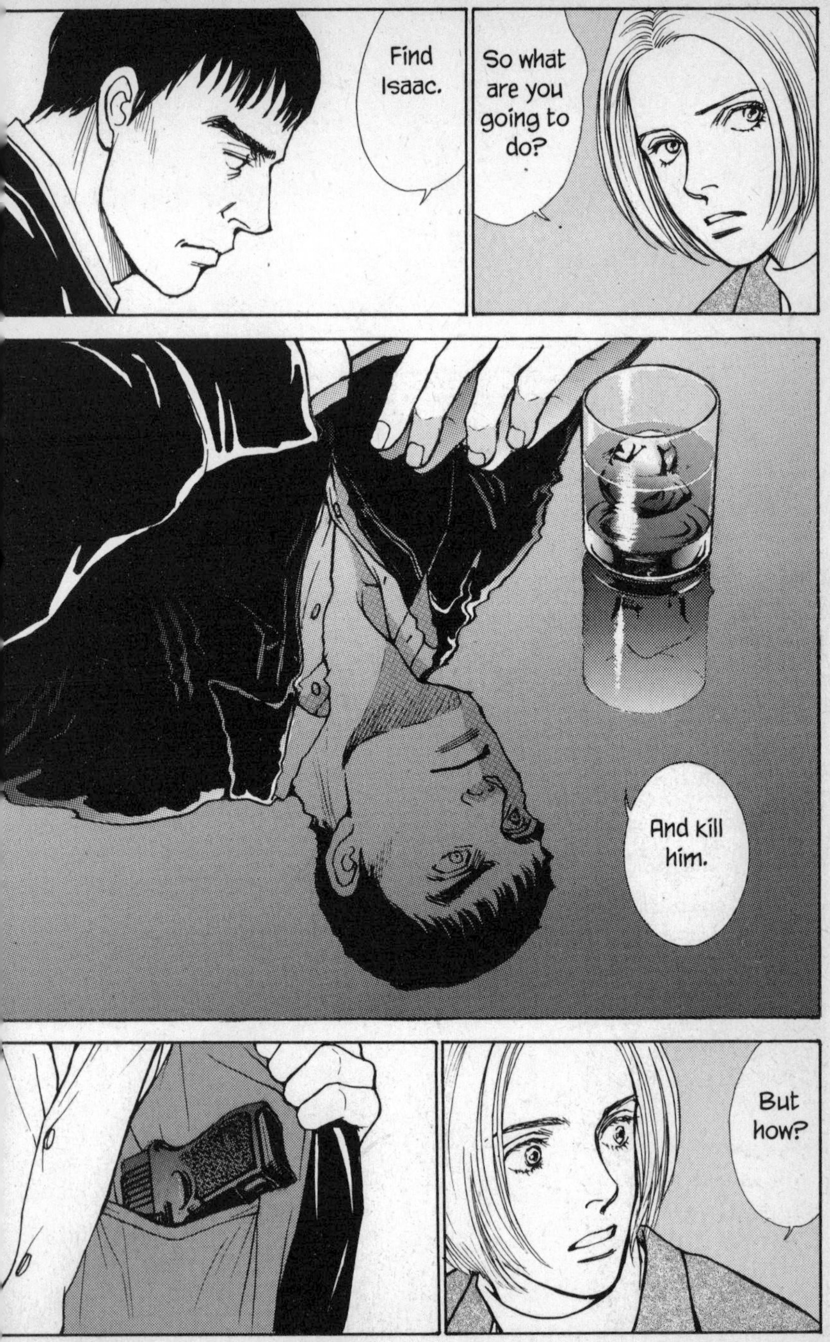

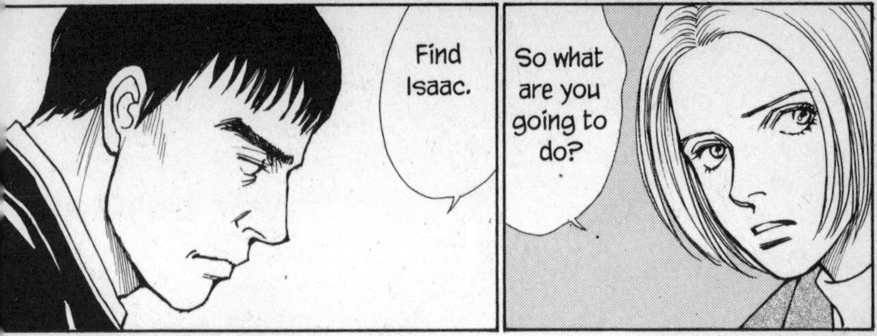

So what are you going to do?
Find Isaac.

And kill him.

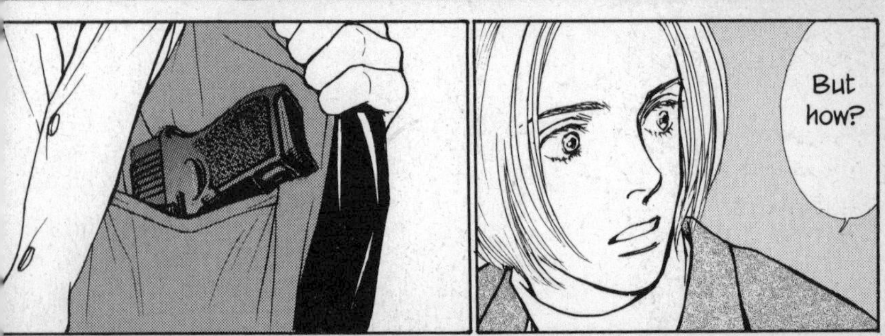

But how?

Are yo serious
Yes, I'm serious. I just can't leave him be.
Whatever it takes, I must destroy him.

Even if it means dying, too.
I must kill him.
This has been my mission since I survived the incident at the lab.

But the reality is I can't do it alone.

I can't get close to Isaac without Shuro.
Shuro can block Isaac's power.

That's why you were asking for Akiba's help?

Do you know where Isaac is?
No...but it's only a matter of time before I do.

I know him. He can't help but make trouble.
I'll find him like I found Shuro. Something strange will happen, some-thing only Isaac could do.

So you were following the fire incident?
Yes. As soon as I read about it, I knew Shuro was involved.
I narrowed my search to the immediate area, looking for the sort of home I thought he'd choose.
I was checking out the Akiba family when I noticed you.

I was relieved to find some-one like me who can resist their powers.
Our kind is rare.
……

Why did Akiba, I mean, Shuro, choose that family?
KARAN カラン
Maybe it was easier to deal with an elderly couple.

But I know why he came to your university.
Keisuke, the head of the Akiba family, is a patient at the university hospital.
Based on my research, I'm pretty sure Keisuke has cancer.

Ryousuke is at the hospital with my husband.

An old man with cancer... I'm not exactly sure why Shuro chose this family—

but he's been staying with them for six months. He must be comfortable.

I think Isaac has found a family, too.

Probably one with a school-age child.

Like Shuro, he's pretending to belong to the family and living a normal life.

Then, one day, someone in his neighborhood will be murdered.

Murdered in a strange way.

Murdered?

TOSS
Is killing Isaac really the only solution?
He's only a child.
He may be a child, but he's still dangerous.
But Akiba isn't dangerous.
And Isaac shares Akiba's genetic makeup. Maybe he could learn to live with humankind?

Impos-sible.
!

Unlike Shuro, his mind was never cultivated.
He'll never under-stand why he should co-exist with us.

Well, that's all your fault.

He was created only to be destroyed.
That's why he can't understand the value of life.

ES.
Shuro.
Isaac.
Ryousuke Akiba.
How weird is it that he was genetically engineered?

402
Keisuke
Akiba

Driving out to the country this weekend?

Yes, Matsuda-kun got his driver's license, so we were talking about going out of town with some of my classmates.

You see, it's autumn and the leaves are changing color... and I thought I'd ask you to come with us.

I'll pass.
What!? Why?
Well, my grandpa's sick.
So I'm not in the mood.
It's just not a good time for me.

......

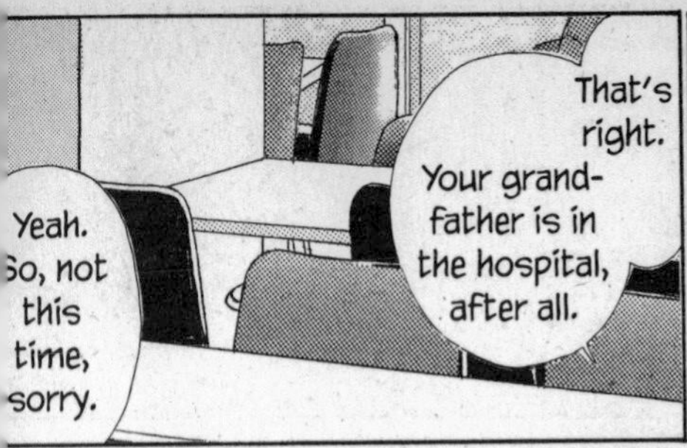
That's right. Your grandfather is in the hospital, after all.
Yeah. So, not this time, sorry.

No worries, I understand. He's been like a father to you.
It's not the right time for hanging out with friends.

Akiba-kun, if there's anything I can do, please ask.
You can come to me anytime.

Okay.
Thank you.

That was cold.

I think she likes you.

I know.

That's right.
I didn't need to tell you that.

So if you know how she feels, you should be a little nicer to her.
Why?
Because she has special feel-ings for you. nd she's cute nd seems like an honest person.

Cute and honest, huh?
クスッ
CHUCKLE

She's preg-nant.
She doesn't know it yet.

I can't even begin to guess who the father is. There are so many images of men around her.
I'd rather not get mixed up in a situation like that.

Seeing so much isn't always a positive thing.
That's what's behind that ironic smile of yours. You know too much about what everyone's thinking.

I wonder if Isaac is smiling, too. Somewhere not far away.

You met Sakaki?

He told me why you and Isaac were created.

And how dangerous Isaac is...
Why did you hide your special powers from Sakaki-san and the other scientists?

For sur-vival.

They never expected we'd have this kind of power.
If the researchers found our powers threatening,
they would have killed us without hesitation.

You're a scientist Don't yo understand?
You know how easy it would be to kill me.
Unlike you humans, we don't have our own identities.
All we have is our code name: ES.

Do you, like Isaac, resent the scientists who created you as an experi-ment?
Are you angry just at Sakaki-san and his colleagues... or do you hate all human-kind?

Humans... huh...
I can't speak for Isaac, but...

...human beings are pretty piti-ful. They can live for only about eighty years or so.

I feel sorry for you guys, but that's about it.

Well...

I'd always thought if I said that to someone, I'd feel better about myself.

But it didn't do much for me after all.

This is a special report.

Kawamoto Takuma-kun, a sixth-grader at Tachibana Elementary School who had been reported missing,

was found dead this morning.

Police have confirmed that they are ruling the boy's death a homicide.

The murder has so far baffled investigators, as just the top of the boy's skull was smashed to pieces.
The type of weapon used in the murder still hasn't been confirmed and police headquarters has been...
CLATTER
!

Holy cow. How do you smash just the *top* of someone's skull?

All these weird murder cases are creeping me out.

Murdered in a strange way...

——The end of #09 An Omen——

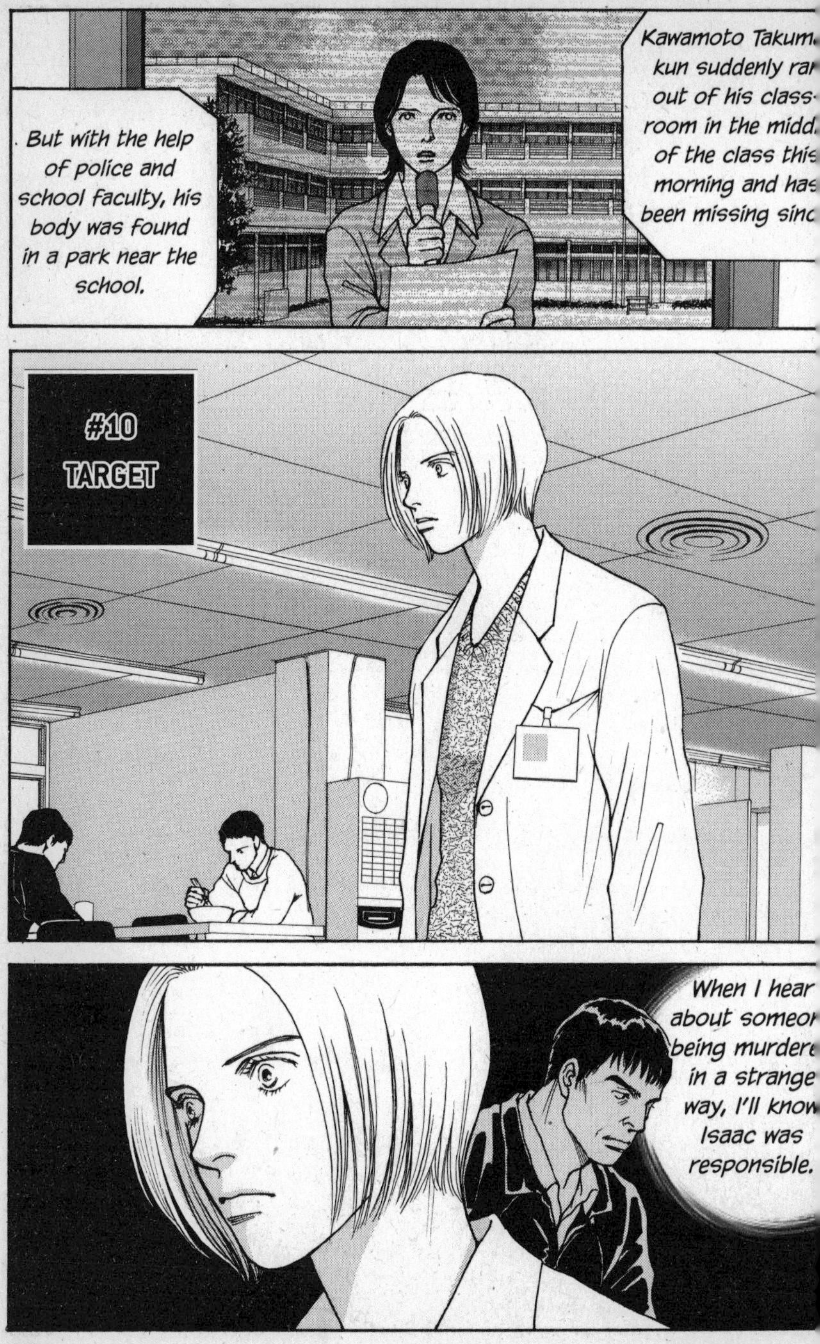

Kawamoto Takum
kun suddenly ra
out of his class-
room in the midd
of the class this
morning and has
been missing sinc
But with the help of police and school faculty, his body was found in a park near the school.

#10 TARGET

When I hear about someo being murdere in a strange way, I'll know Isaac was responsible.

BEEP
ピ
ッ
BEEP
ピ
ッ
BEEP
ピ
ッ

And wh
will yo
do aft
you te
Sakak
about
it?

Do you even
know what
you're doing?
Sakaki's not
dealing with a
ordinary kid.
If you help
Sakaki, Isaac
will regard you
as an enemy.

Isaac sees
everyone,
besides him-
self, as mere
worms.
If you were
to become
his target,
he will surely
kill you.

What a surprise.
You're worried about me?

I didn't think you cared about other people.

But that doesn't mean you'll help us, does it?

That makes sense. We scientists took advantage of you and Isaac for our research.
We can't ask you for help now...

But...

And to you, we're just an inferior species.
Killing one of us would be just like killing a worm.

We still have our pride.
If my life was in danger, I'd fight to save myself. That's what I call being alive.

I haven't personally done any harm to Isaac.
But so long as he sees humans as worthless, I see him as a menace.

This isn't just Sakaki-san's problem.

Isaac is my enemy, too.

THE LIGHT FOR THE SPIRIT OF THE DEAD

What do you think? Have you seen Isaac yet?
No, not yet.

Call it mysterious or weird or what have you, never in my life have I seen a dead body like this one.

But I'm sur
Isaac was involved wit
this murder

I called in some favors and acquired the results o the autopsy.

And, just as I thought, the murder was highly unusual.

So the skull was smashed to pieces
That's correct, but...

Only the brain and the top part of the skull were smashed. There were no other external injuries.
How can I describe it?
Okay, look at this.

Soy Sauce-Flavored Rice Cracker
The skull looked like this.
Soy Sauce-Flavored Rice Cracker
SMASH
It makes me sick to think about Isaac.
......
I've got to find him soon.

Detec
tive
Hotta..
I know that detective. I'm going to talk to him!
!

Don't worry, Isaa
doesn't know who I am.
I'll pretend that I know the family of the victim, and they'll give me the inside scoop.

Hello,
Hotta-sa

Dr. Kujyou!?

Never thought I'd see you in a place like this.
Dr. Kujyou, did you know the victim's family?
Ah...
yes, kind of.

I was just wondering what exactly happened before and after Takuma-kun was killed?
Here's what we know.

On the day of the murder, the victim was in class. Just like a normal school day.
But during class, he all of a sudden screamed and ran from the room.

The boy was later found dead in the park near the school.

We have no
suspects
and no
murder
weapon.
And we don't understand how exactly the victim was murdered.

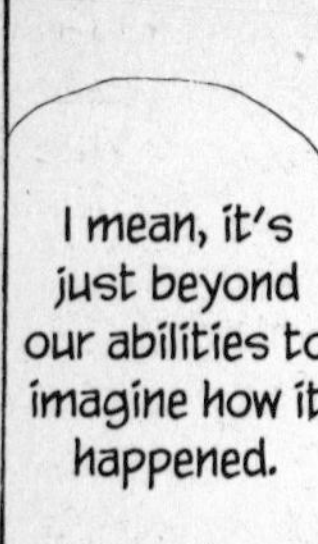

I mean, it's just beyond our abilities to imagine how it happened.

All we know is that
school janitor who passed by Takuma-kun in the hallway a
he was fleeing the classroom heard the boy screaming something.
What was it?

Takuma-kun kept looking over his shoulder and screaming "Get away from me" as if something was chasing him ...

But the janitor said that nobody else was there.

......

Has Takuma-kun's school recently hosted any new transfer students?
uh!?

A transfer student?
Or any kind of new student.

No, I haven't heard any-thing like that.
Besides, I don't see what it has to do with this case.
Ah...
Um.
I guess you're right.

Mr. Hot you hav call fro head-quarte
I'll see you later then.
Pardon me.

I heard you ask the officer...

...something about a new student?

!

Ah... I ought to introduce myself. My name is Kojima and I was Takuma Kawamoto's teacher.

I couldn't help but overhear your conversation just now...

You were Takuma-kun's teacher?

Then you know what happened right before Takuma-kun's death?

Yes, that's why I wanted to talk to you.

GASP

GASAH

BATT
!

Iwamura...

What are you doing over there?
Your mother will scold you if she catches you out wandering again.

Who was that?
One of my students.
She's a year younger than Takuma-kun and was in my class last year.

We're out in the open here.

If you're available, could we meet again and talk about this tomorrow?
!

All right, tomorrow then.
My name is Kujyou and I'm a researcher at Touhou Medical University.
Please contact me any-time.
SHIVER ブル
SHIVER ブル
SHIVER ブル
I'll call you late to set up the meeting time and location

......

——The end of #10 Target——

#11
A VICTIM

!

GRABB

ガッ

GABAH
UWAH.

Do you really think that teacher knows about Isaac?
Yes...
He acted so strangely, like he was afraid of something.
Maybe he's like us, and Isaac can't influence him.
Anyway, let's hear what he has to say.
Perhaps he can help us.

This is Sakaki-san. He also wants to hear your story.

I'm sorry behaved so oddly the other day.

If you don't mind, could you tell us about the day of the murder?

!
On that day, the day Takuma-kun died, some-one visited our classroom.

It was just at the beginning of first period.

The door opened and there was a boy standing there.

Th...the strange thing was that every-one ignored him, just as if they couldn't see him.
Everyone besides me.

I didn't know how to respond. I was nervous, but this boy ignored me. He went up to Takuma and placed his hand on his shoulder, and right then...

GYAAAAAH.
CLATTER
Get away from me.

Every-one run!
Run!

Takuma fled the classroom as if pursued by monsters. And not long after that, he was found dead.

What about the boy who visited him?
Did he also disappear that day?

He comes to school every day.
And acts as if he's one of our students.

But I've never seen him before.

He's never been a student at the school.

I have no idea how he got in.

just can't believe nobody's oticed he's retending to e one of our students.

But what I specially an't understand is...

How is something like this even possible?
Everyone but me has simply accepted his existence.
Kojima-sensei...
They all think that I've gone crazy but I'm perfectly sane. I know my own students' faces.
Kojima sensei please calm down.
GASP
はっ…
Please relax, Kojima-sensei,
I... I'm sorry.
And who is this student?
Um...I think that he is...

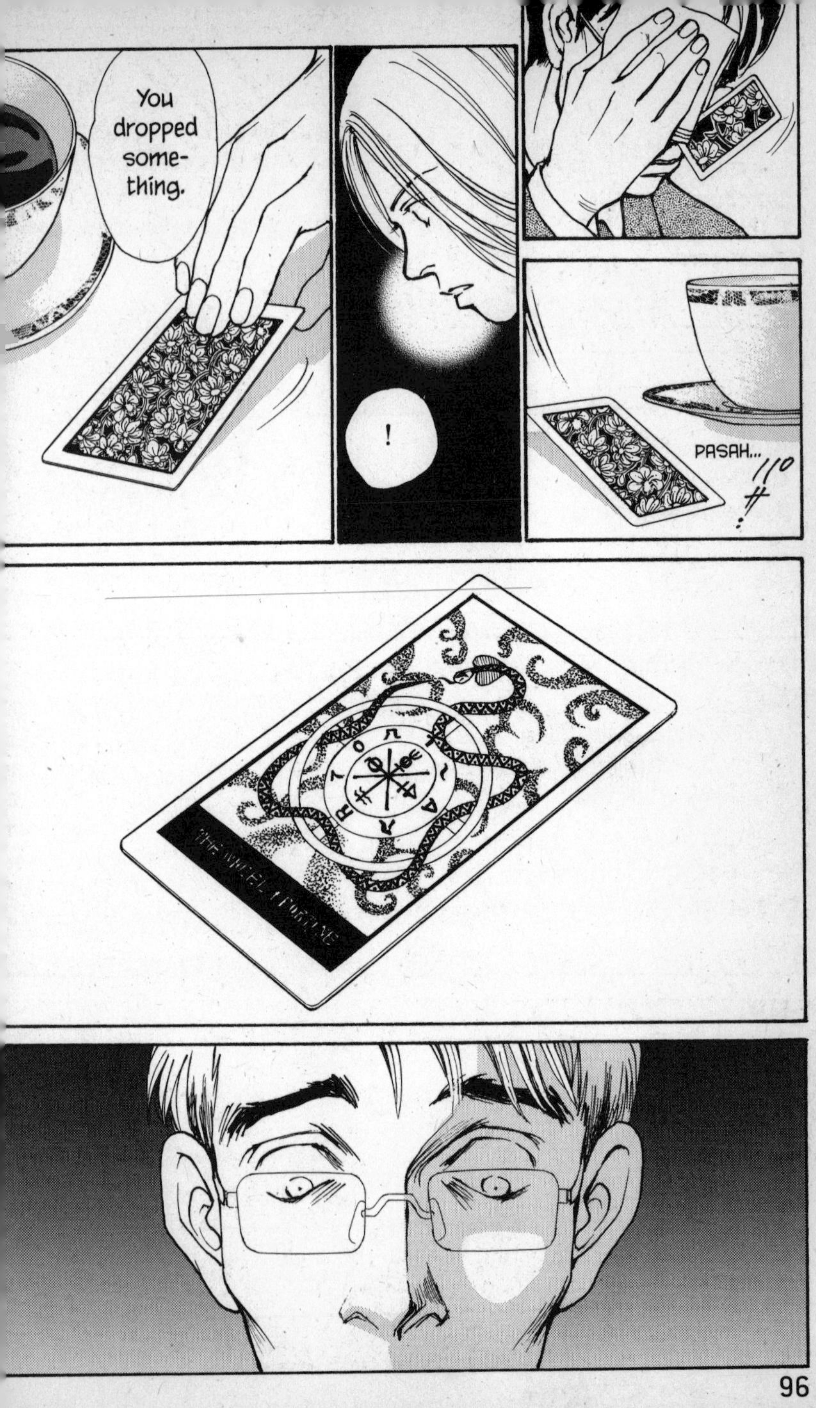

You dropped something.

!

PASAH...

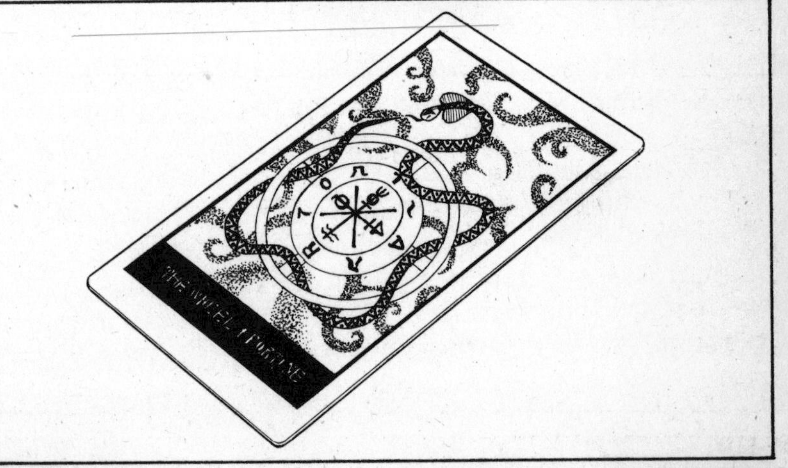

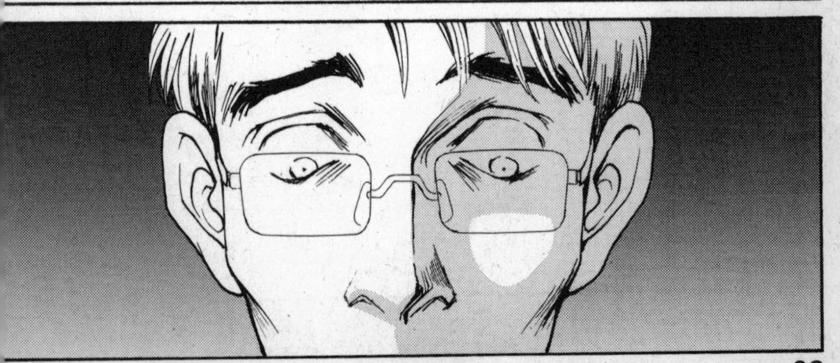

CLATTER
The Ring of Ouroboros? This is a tarot card.
Th... this is intimidation.
He's put this in my pocket to scare me.
I...I don't like snakes since I was a kid, I've hated them
It's him. He's doing this to me.

UWAAAH.

Kojima-san!?

Kojima-sensei!?

Kojima-
san, what
wrong!?
!
HEE...
地下鉄
SUBWAY
青山三丁目
Aoyama 3rd Street
Hee.
!
GAH

PANT
PANT
STAGGER
STAGGER
FALLEN
!
BEEP

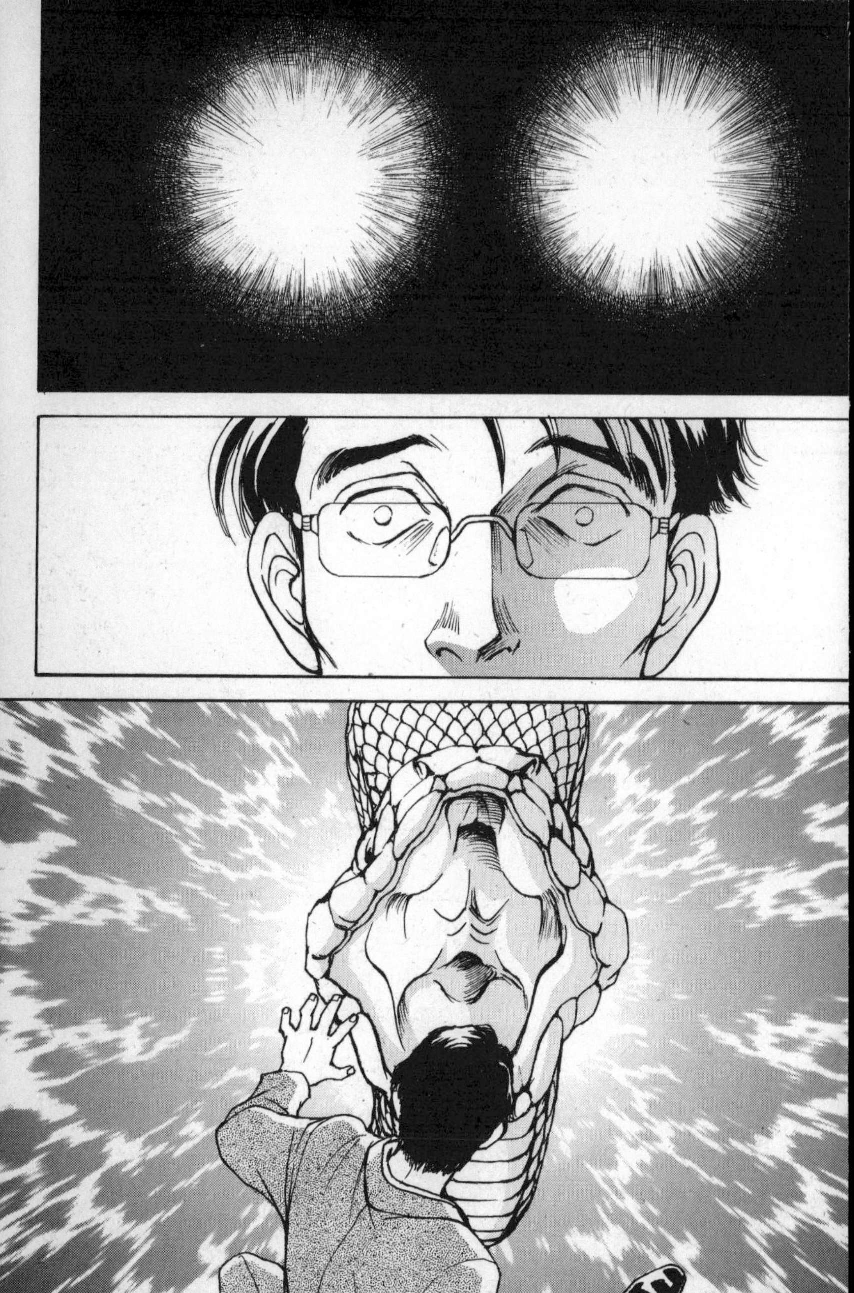

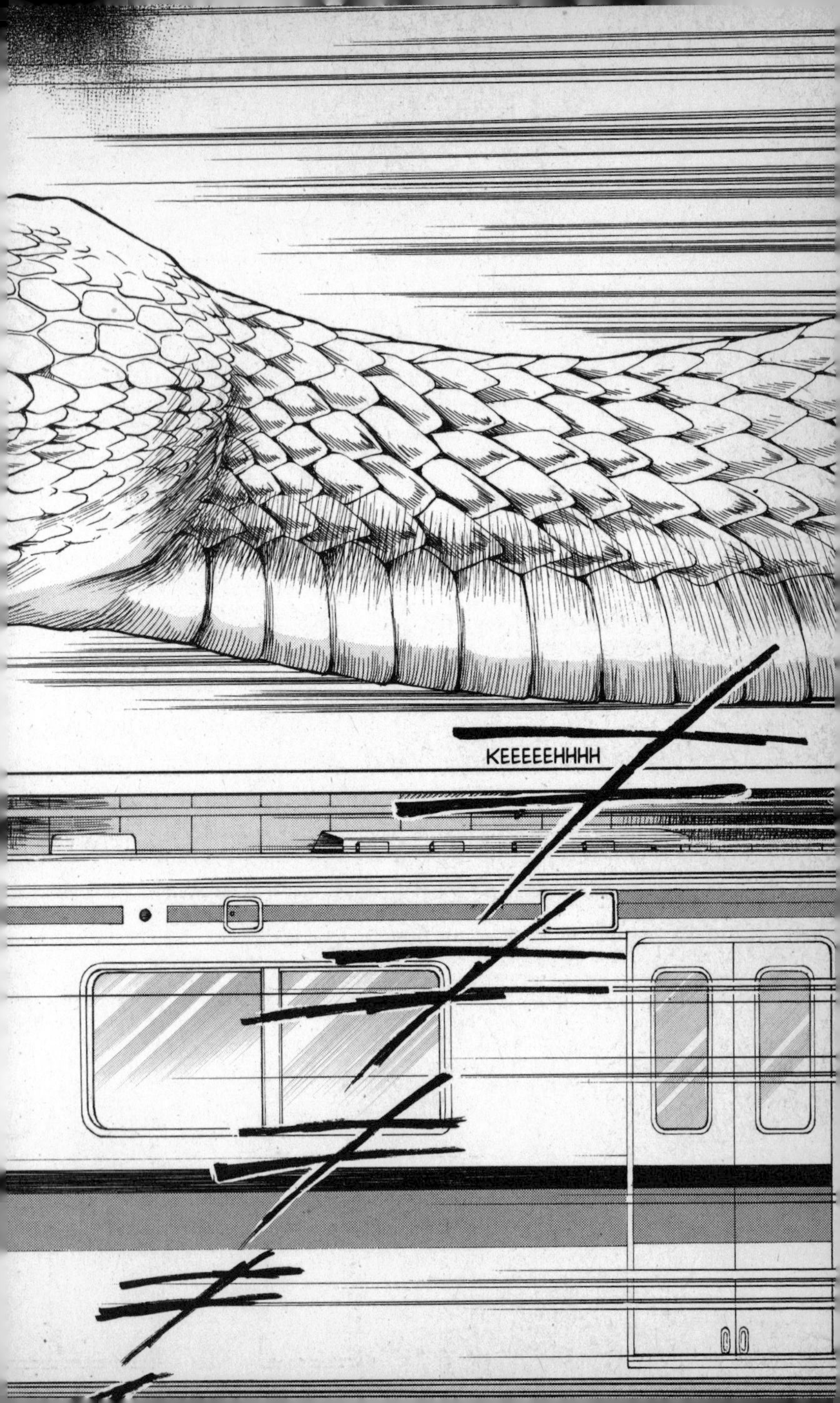
KEEEEEHHHH

Oh, no! Someone just got hit by the train.

Holy crap...

—The end of #11 A Victim—

#12
APPEARANCE

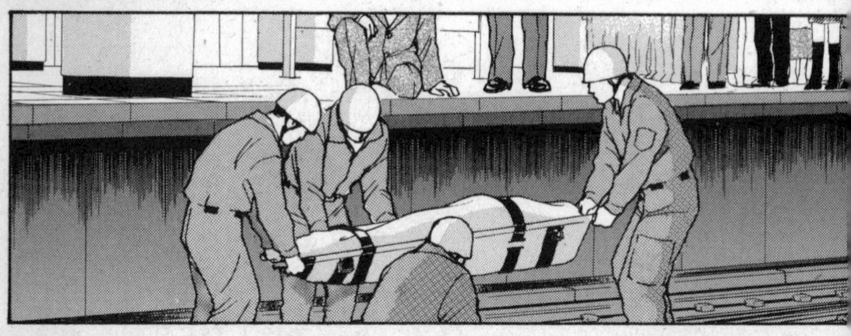

......

How could this have happened?

Isaac murdered him.

But this made it crystal clear.
There's no doubt that Isaac goes to this school.

And he knows that we're on to him.

SCHOOLTEACHER COMMITS SUICIDE

Um...
My name is Kujyou. I'm here to burn incense for the soul of your husband.

Oh, we spoke on the phone earlier. Please come in.

Yuri-chan, thank you for stopping by today.

I'm very sorry to hear about your hus band.
……

I know my husband didn't commit suicide.

He had moments of weakness, but know he would nev kill himself.
I know he felt badly about his student's death. But he just wasn't the suicidal type.

I can't tell her the truth. It would just confuse her.
And even if I told her why her hus-band died and what's been happening at the school...
...it vouldn't ease her pain. he'd just ndanger herself, like Kojima-san did.

That girl. From the funeral.
So...the girl I saw ealier...she a student Tachibana Elementar right?
Yes, her name is Iwamura Yuri-chan.
My husband was her fourth grade teacher.
She came here by herself to visit?
Yes, actually.
She wanted to apologize to my husband. That's why she came.
Apologize?
I wond why
Well, I just don't know.
But she was crying and saying that my husband died because of her.

Um...I must be going.
Oh!? But I haven't served you any tea yet.

I wonder why she would say that it was her fault?
I'm not sure, but she said something about a snake card.

Please don't worry about it.

校
前
Iwamura... Yuri-chan?

You must be Iwamura Yuri-chan.
Do you remember me?
We met at Kawamoto Takuma-kun's funeral.

Kojima-sense
wife told me t
you visited s
that you cou
apologize to
sensei.
What did you want to apolo-gize to him about?
......

Because I wa
the one who
told "him" th
sensei was
talking to yo
That's why sensei was killed just like that upper classman, Takuma.

He was killed...
...by whom?
Tomo-kun.

But not the real Tomo-kun.

I don't know who he really is.

But I like this Tomo-kun better.
The old Tomo-kun was mean and I didn't like him.
I didn't like Takuma either. Nobody liked him so it's okay that he's dead.

But I feel bad for Kojima-sensei a little bit.
He didn't do anything wrong.

But Tomo-kun said that it's better that he's dead.
If he was alive, he'd do things he shouldn't.

Is that why you put that card into Kojima-sensei's pocket?
Tomo-kun asked me to do it.
Because Sensei hated snakes.

Tomo-kun still goes to your school, right?

Can you tell me his full name?

Tomoya Takaoka.

Hey, you go to Tachibana, don't you?
So when u graduate, u'll come to junior high. So give us me money. nd when ou come o our hool, we'll ake re of ou.

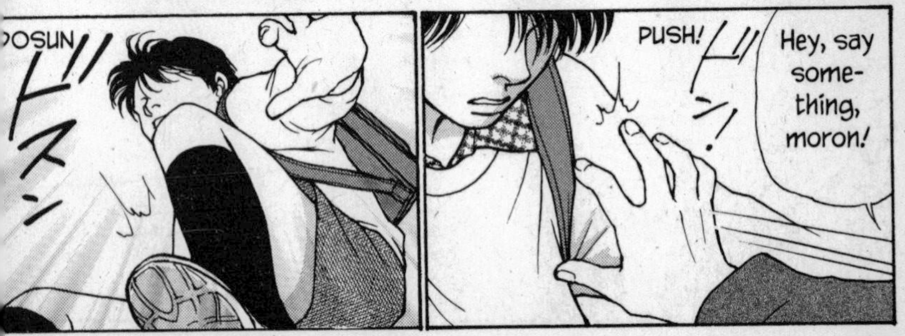
Hey, say some-thing, moron!
PUSH!
OSUN

Hey, you guys, discipline him.

GRABB
!
Wha...what the hell are you doing? Stop!
Why are you attacking me?
Stop it!
Hey!
I told you to stop!

MISHI
MISHI
GISHI
!
GUKI

—The end of #12 Appearance—

#13 A DISASTER

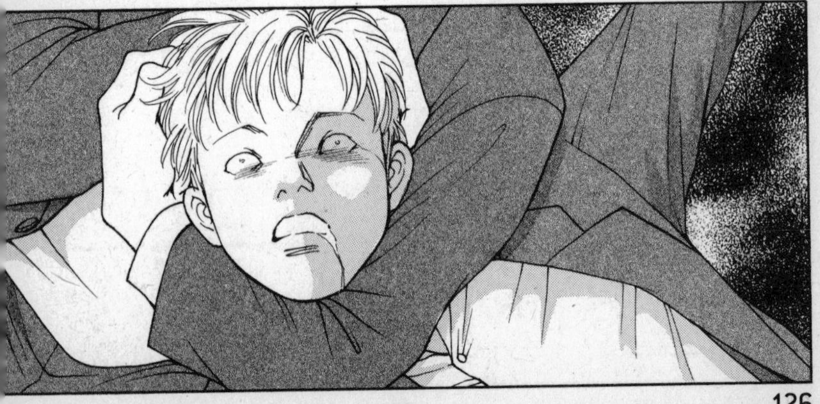

KYAAAAAHH.

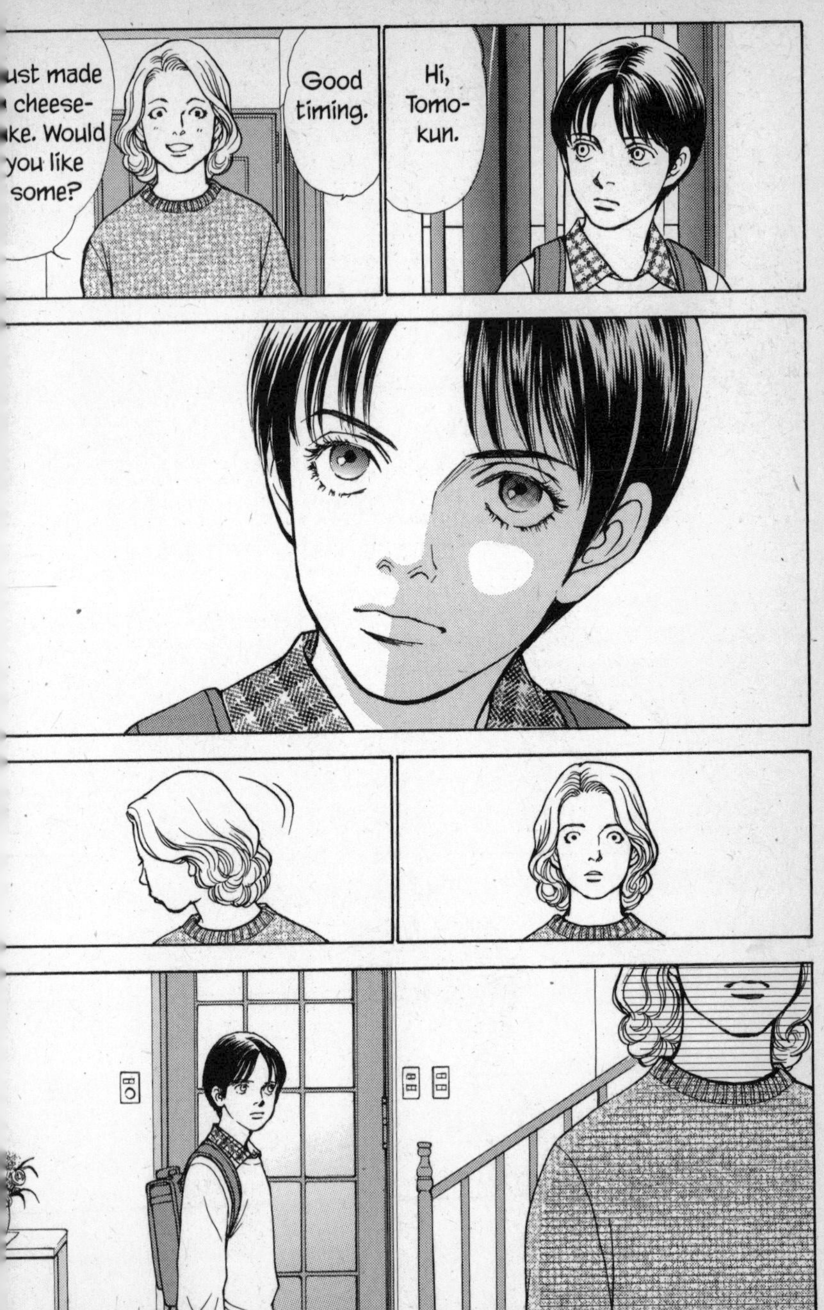
Hi, Tomo-kun.
Good timing.
ust made cheese- ke. Would you like some?

DOSAH
ドサ…

VIII
PASAH
THE STRENGTH
Sakaki...

PASAH
Mine Kujyou.
THE JUSTICE

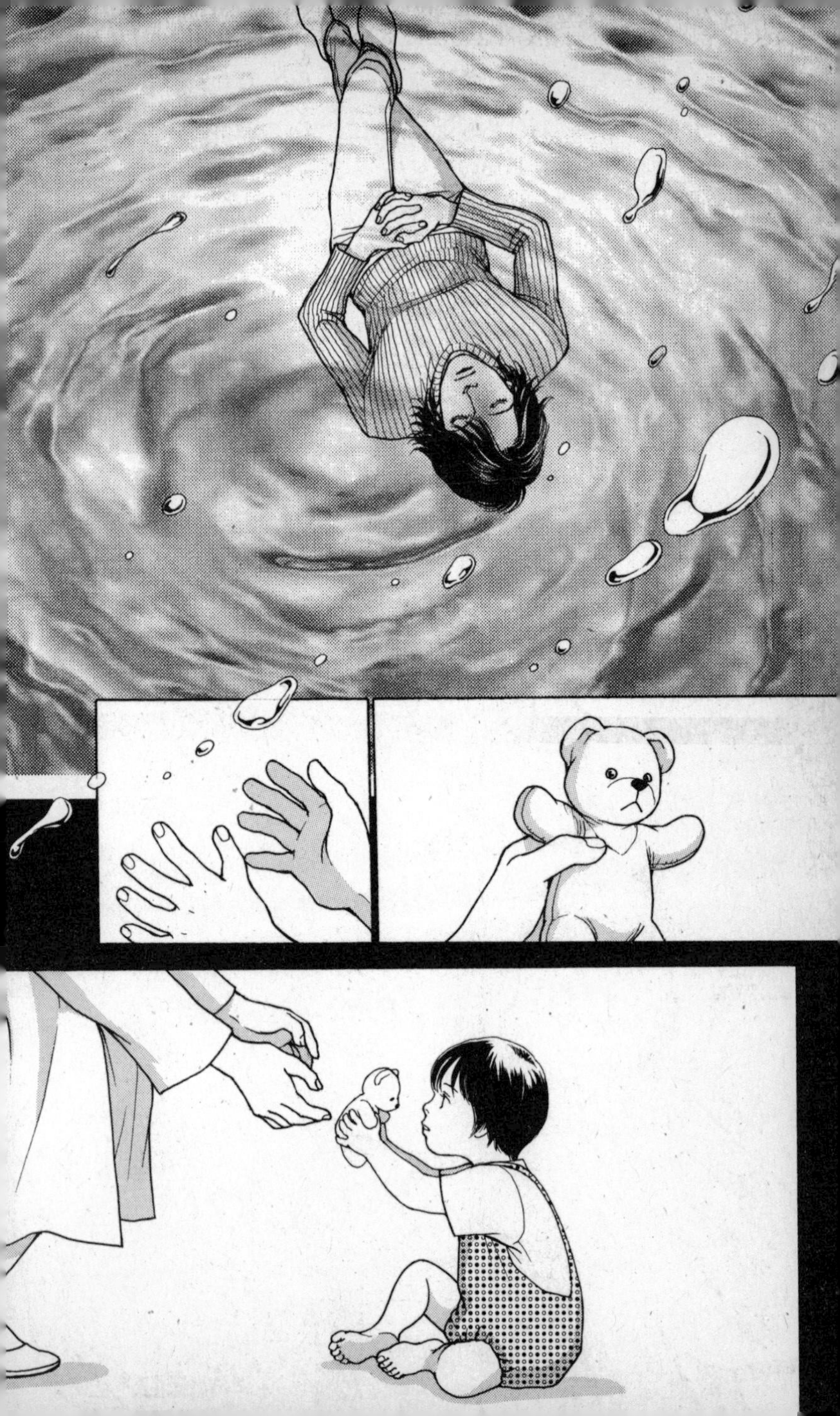

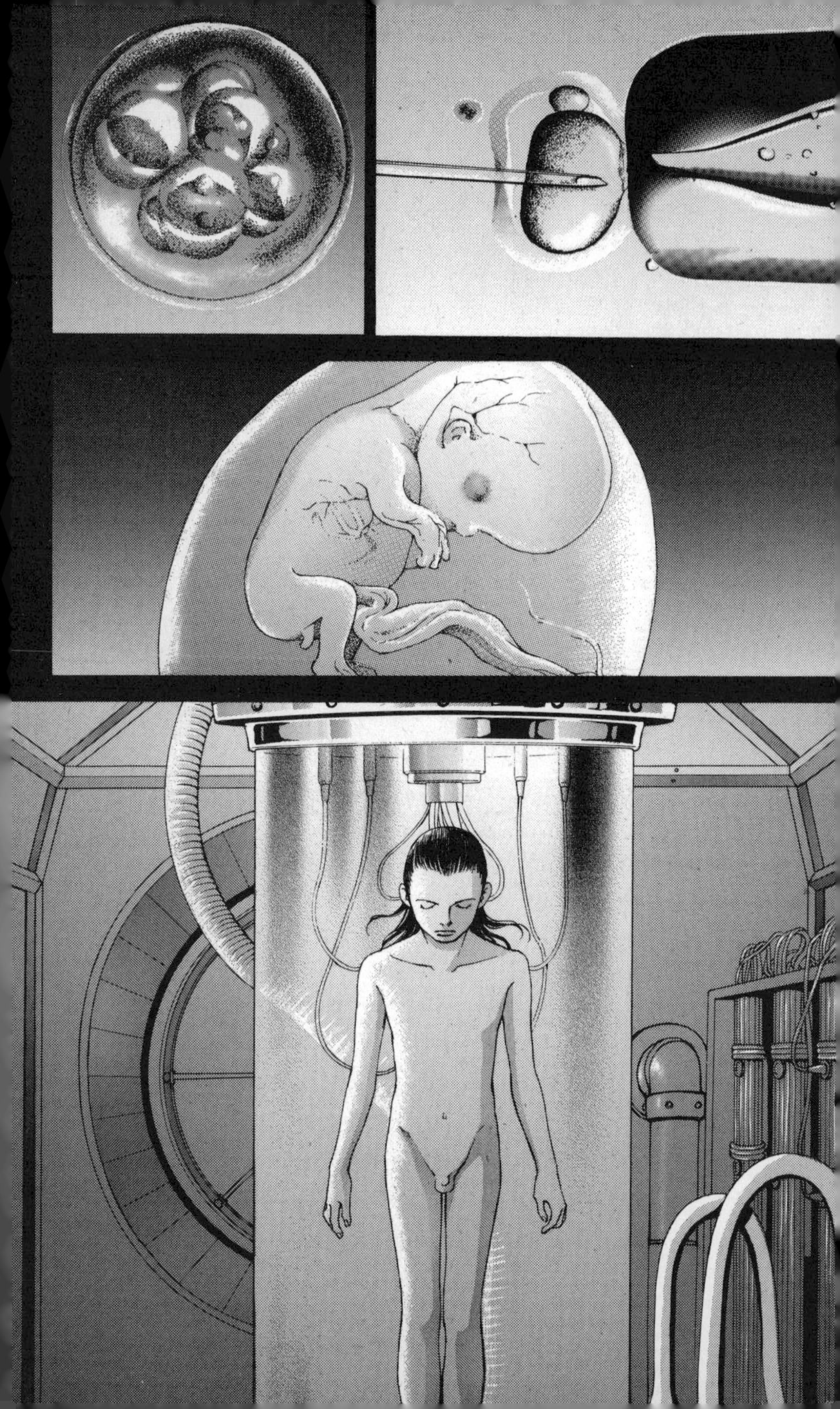

GATAN
!
Ryou-suke.
Dinner's ready. Come on down.

Ryou-
suke.

Isaac is pretendin to be a boy name Tomoya Takaoka.
Yes, it was one month ago when he appeared as Tomoya Takaoka.
It's very likely that's when the real Tomoya was killed.

I get that Isaa killed Tomoya i order to steal hi identity. Why did he kill Takuma Kawamoto?
......
Yuri Iwamura was involved.
?

The day he was murdered, Takuma bullied Yuri-chan.
Takuma was a well-known problem student.
/henever was up- et about some- ing, he'd eat up a student. le was a vild kid.
Takuma was killed by his favorite video game monster.
A monster that kills by smashing its victim's head with its hands.
omo- kun told ne so.

So we know where he is. What are we going to do?
He can't really go anywhere but home and school.
He's mostly active during the day. But because he's a child, we could get in trouble if we approach him without reason.

Could we use Yuri Iwamura?
!

Wait! Sakaki-san.
You're saying you want to involve Yuri-chan?
Yuri can resist Isaac's powers. And he seems to trust her.
If we can approach him by using her—

She's totally innocent.
This could be dangerous. What if some-thing were to happen to her?

PASSA-T
JR. HIGH STUDENT DIES IN ACCIDENT

This student died yesterday.
He died while wrestling with three of his friends for fun.

It doesn't matter who we involve, because every human being is already involved.

If Isaac gets out of control, our whole society will collapse.

And since Shuro won't help us, we have to find a way to save ourselves.
Could you persuade Yuri wamura to draw Isaac out?

COULD YOU PERSUADE YURI IWAMURA TO DRAW ISAAC OUT?

14
AN
INTENTION

Yuri-
chan.

Hell
Do you remem-ber me?
If you don't mind, I'd like to speak to you for a mo-ment. Is that okay with you?

I'd like to talk to you about Tomoya Takaoka... Tomo-kun.
Are you okay with the fact that he's not the real Tomo-kun?

Yep.
He's a nicer person than the old Tomo-kun.

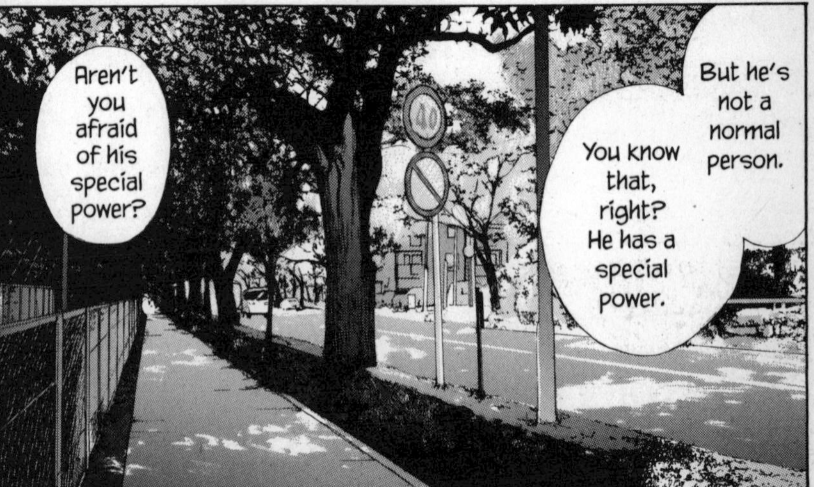
But he's not a normal person.
You know that, right? He has a special power.
Aren't you afraid of his special power?

No, because Tomo-ku gets rid of only bad people.
He wouldn't hurt me.
But he might hurt you one day.
Just like he killed Kojima-sensei.
You know that Kojima-sensei wasn't a bad person, right?
He wasn't bad but he wasn't any good either.
He never really punished Kawamoto-kun.

There's a dog that lives in the backyard of the school. Shiro. Takuma-kun put out his eye.
He was shooting targets with a pinball and hit Shiro's eye.
Kojima-sensei didn't even scold Takuma-kun.

Satoko-chan loved Shiro, too. She was crying so hard. But Sensei did nothing.
ULTRAVIOLET
So I went up to Takuma-kun and told him to apologize to Satoko-chan and Shiro.
So he hit me. Many times.

Tomo-kun saw Takuma-kun beating me up and we talked about it.

He said he'd kill Takuma-kun for me.

And that's why you took revenge on him?

So I told him to go ahead and kill him.

In the grown-up world, bad people get punished, don't they?
Bad people should be killed, right?
Tomo-kun and I aren't doing anything wrong, right?

I like Tomo-kun better now.

Yes, there are truly bad people in this world.
I know how you feel. But killing is never the right thing to do.
People who think it's the right way to solve a problem are wrong.

You know that's true, because you went to Kawamoto-kun's funeral.
You also went to Kojima-sensei's house.

Why is it wrong
A lot of people are glad that Kawamoto-kun is dead.

But some people are sad about it, too.

And he must have killed the real Tomo-kun in order to take his place.
He's a dangerous person who would do anything to get what he wants.

His real name is Isaac.

He comes from a very different background and has a different upbringing from us. He has a very dangerous power.

Tomo-kun is someone who can't be allowed in our society.
If he keeps living among us, he could destroy the whole world.
......

Then where should Tomo-kun live?
Is there a home for Tomo-kun?

Right now someone is lookin for him.
He's known Tomo-kun since he was born and wants to bring him back to where he came from.
But Tomo-kun doesn't want to go back, so he's running away.

That's why I need your help.
!
Me?
Tomo-kun seems to trust you.
Please make up a reason to bring Tomo-kun to the person who's waiting for him.
You want me to lie to him?

We don't have another choice. Only you can help us.

Since he can read other people's minds, you're our only hope.

s it really best for Tomo-kun to go back to where he came from?

Is that really the best thing for Tomo-kun?

There's an abandoned factory near the school. If we can lure him there, I can kill him without any interference.

Yes.

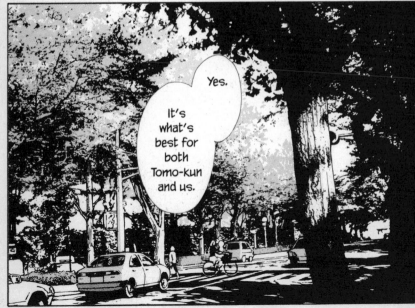

It's what's best for both Tomo-kun and us.

Yes, it went well. Yuri-chan agreed to go along with it.
I'm glad to hear that.
If Isaac does as she says, we may very well be able to capture him.
No, we've got to capture him no matter what it takes.
....
Sakaki-san, promise me one thing.
?
Promise me you won't kill Isaac in front of Yuri-chan.

I'm sorry, but I can't make that promise.

...I can't guarantee Yuri's safety.

Just think about who I'm dealing with. I don't have time to worry about that. And i worse comes to worst...

What do you mean? She's innocent!
And she's like us—she's immune to Isaac's power!
I have no choice.

Think about how many victims there could be in Isaac's future. This is our only option.

But...

Sakaki-san?

Sakaki-san.

BEEP

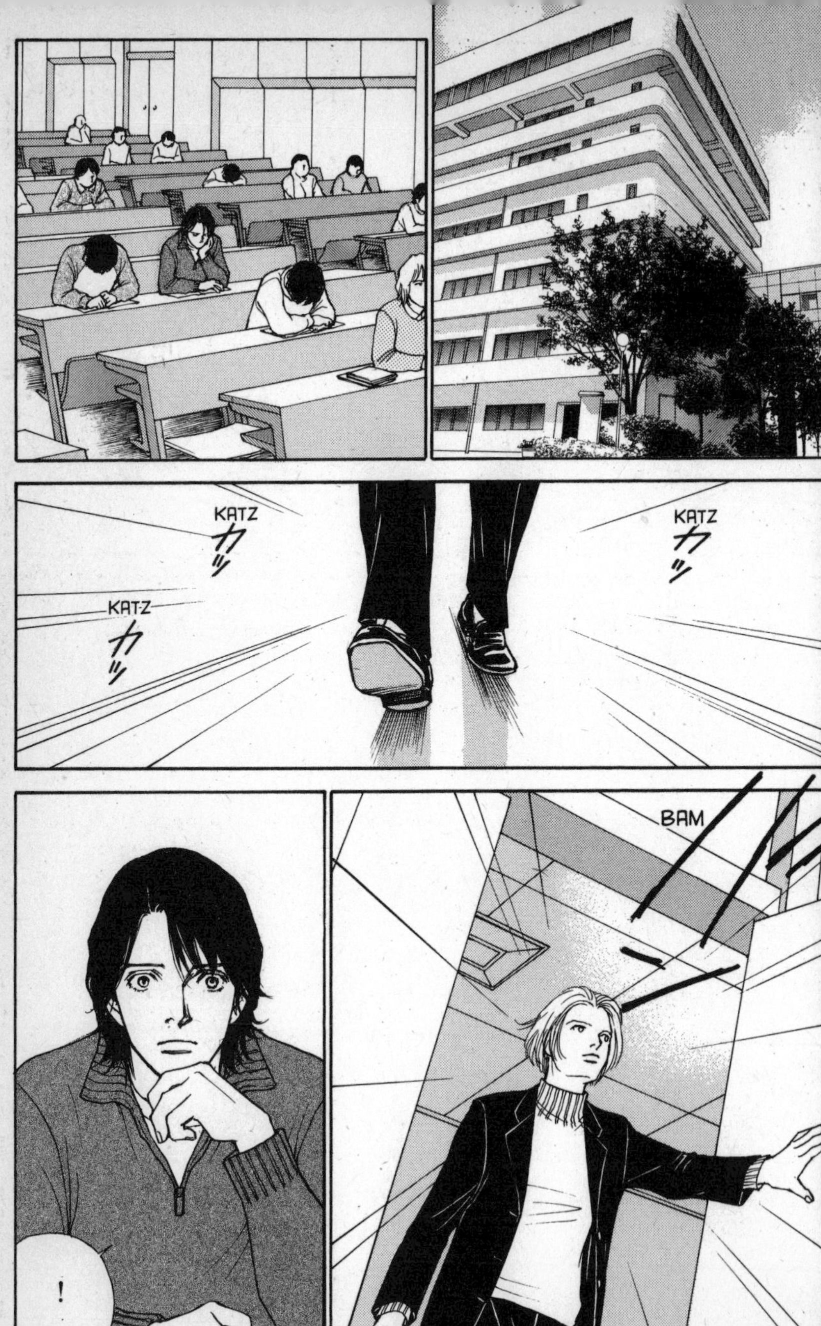
KATZ
カッ
KATZ
カッ
KAT-Z
カッ
BAM
!

Akiba-kun, do me a favor.
Please come with me.

—The end of #14 An Intention—

#15
A TRAP

Right now Sakaki-san is heading to a final battle wit
Isaac.
But I can't imagine he'll succeed by himself.

Please follow me.
What's going on over there? This is a class-room!

I told you again and again. This has nothing to do with me.
Isaac is Sakaki's problem, not mine.

See, you're only making trouble. It's not like you.

Why don't you leave quietly before they throw you out?

Wait.

Hey, you! Leave my classroom immediately!

This isn't just Sakaki-san's problem.
It threatens all of society. The society you want to belong to.
It has already claimed victims.

Today an innocent little girl might be next.
And I'm going to do everything I can to stop it.
What are you doing?

What are you thinking? A class is in session here!

!

Please leave.

Please help us.

I don't want that little girl to be involved anymore.

JAKI

ジャキ

This way, Tomo-kun.

This is my secre place.

It's where I hide my treasure.

......

JARI

This way.
de it the ck.

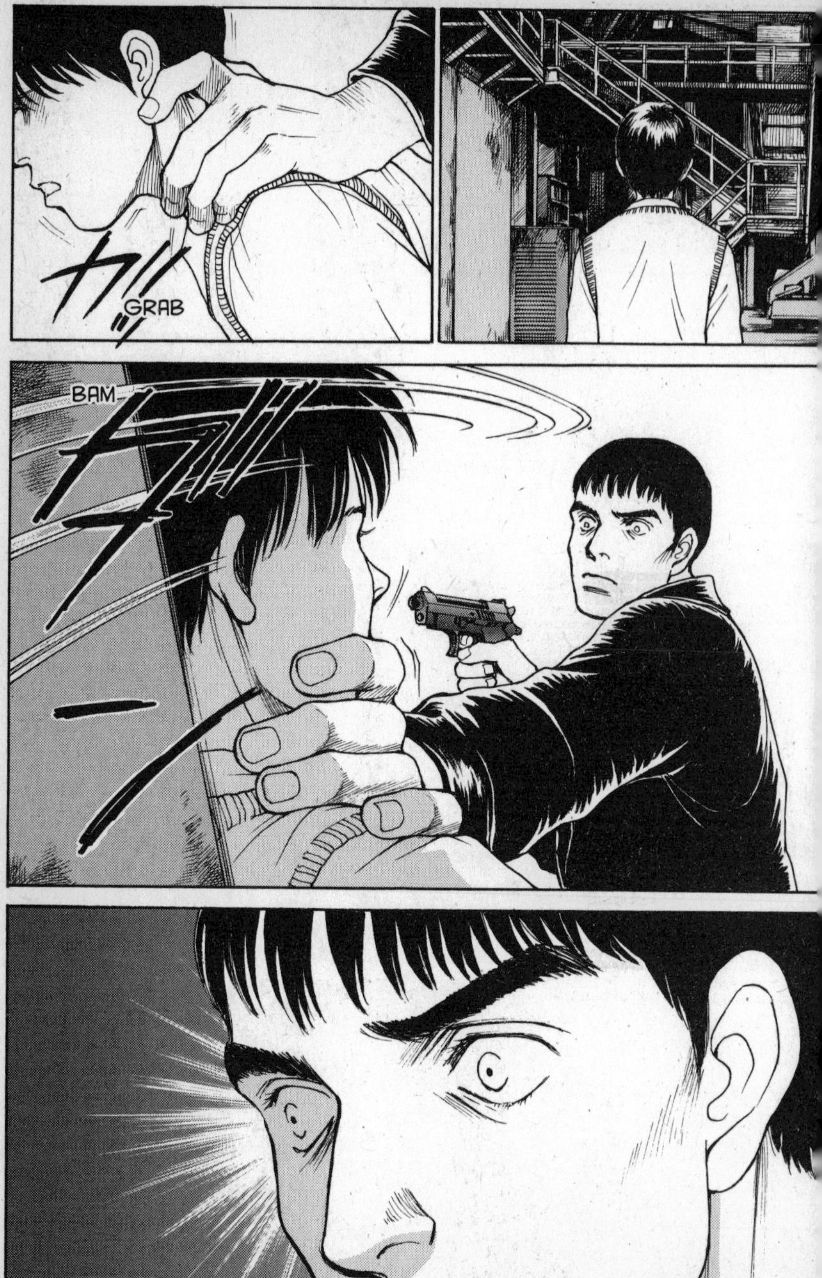

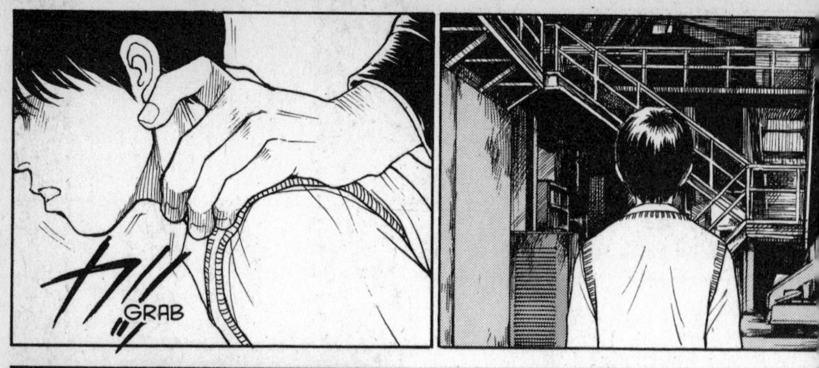

BAM

ou're ot...
Isaac.
CHUCKLE
CHUCKLE
CHUCKLE
!
What an idiot.
You fell for it.

Sakaki.

You're the one who survived.

BAM

TING

Wait,
Isaac.

Holy
crap!

Wait.

GASP...
はっ..

POW
!
POW
POW
POW

TING
TING
DASH
TING
Are you seri-ous?
This totally sucks.

PANT
はあ
PANT
はあ…
BATAH
バタ
BATAH
バタ
BATAH
バタ

TAP
ポン

CHA-K
チャッ

!

Good thing I made it in time.

—The end of #15 A Trap—

#16
ESCAPE
Kujyou-san invited me. She said you needed my help.

Miss Kujyou did?

Akiba-kun.
Akiba-kun, please help Sakaki-san.

Hold on. Don't mis-understand me. I didn't come here for you.
I came here to help a girl named Yuri.

You came here because Miss Kujyou asked you to?

Though it does seem as if you fell for the trap Yuri set for you.

It's amazing how smart kids are.
ANNOYED
Oh well. Looks like Isaac has a power-ful partner who he can trust.

Not to make excuses, but I didn't think a girl like her would deceive us.
And she's the same type of human as Kujyou and me.
But thanks to Yuri, I could have been shot to pieces by those cops.

!
Yuri and the substitute have already escaped.
Maybe we should make a break for it, too.

Wait a minute, the substi-tute...if you knew about that...
...does that mean you saw the whole thing?

Because I didn't think you'd fall for their trap so easily.

Basi cally
Then why didn't you catch Isaac?
Because I'm here only be-cause Kujyou-san asked me to protect you and Yuri.
Then why didn't you stop him before the police sur-rounded me?

If you think about it, it was pretty easy to figure out. Plus it was amusing watching you deal with it.

I HATE YOU!
!

They're over here.
Dammit.

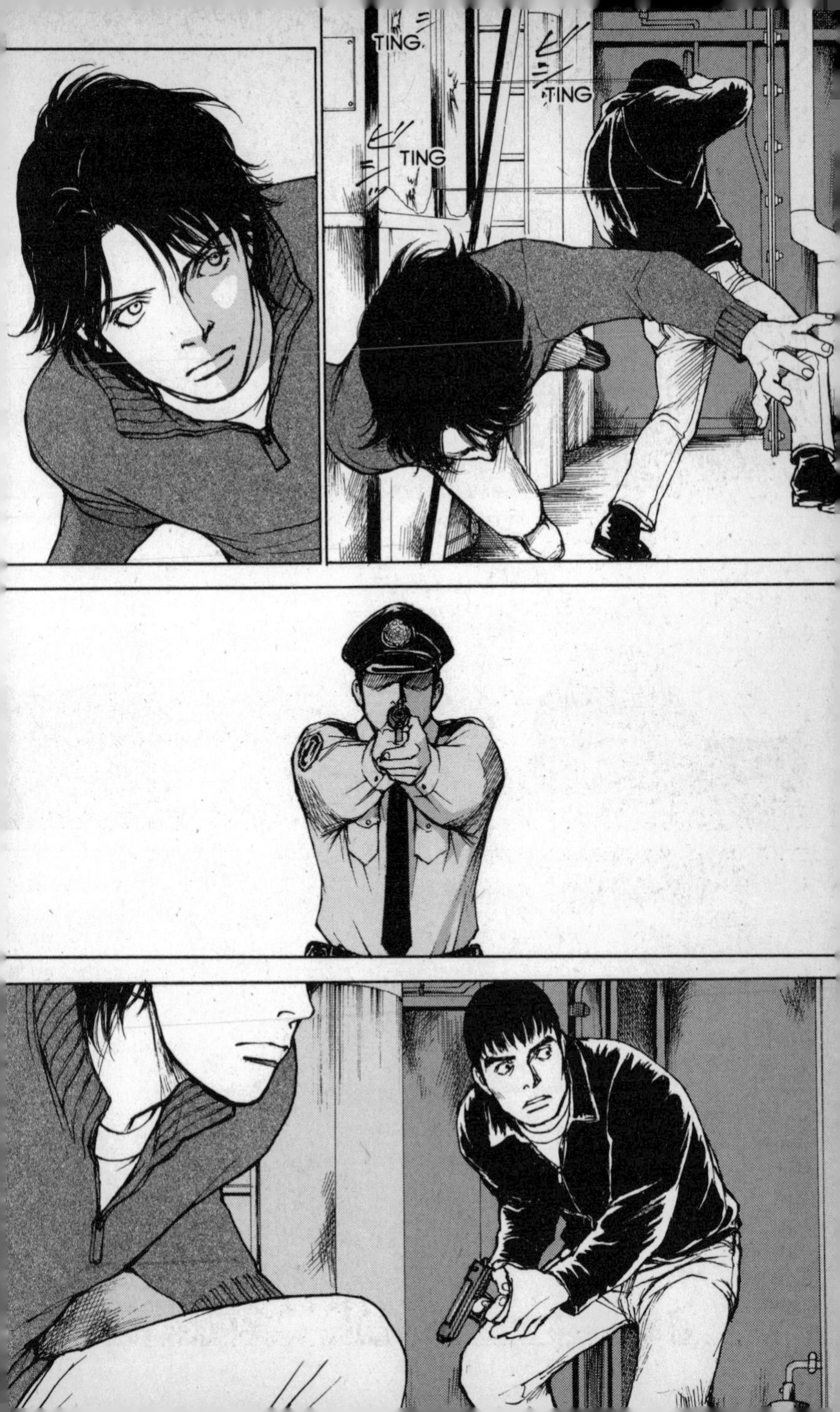

TING

TING

TING

GASP
ギリょっ

Did you stop him from breathing, too?
If I hadn't, he would have shot us.

But won't he die if we leave him like that?
That's a terrible thing to do.
Then tell me what I should do.
If I put him back to normal, it would only confuse him.
!

Just change his target to someone else.
Make them shoot each other.
Are you serious!?
They'll start killing each other.
Don't worry. Japanese police officers are trained to shoot at the target's hands and feet.

TAP
I'll see about that.

TURN

BAM
BAM
BAM
BAM
BAM

Any more bright ideas? They're ready for a fight.
Besides, I can still feel Isaac's presence. They'll just get even angrier.
Hell, at this point, just let them shoot each other up.
Once they run out of bullets, we'll make our escape.

Do you think that'll work?
I don't care. Just do it.

POW
TING
POW
POW

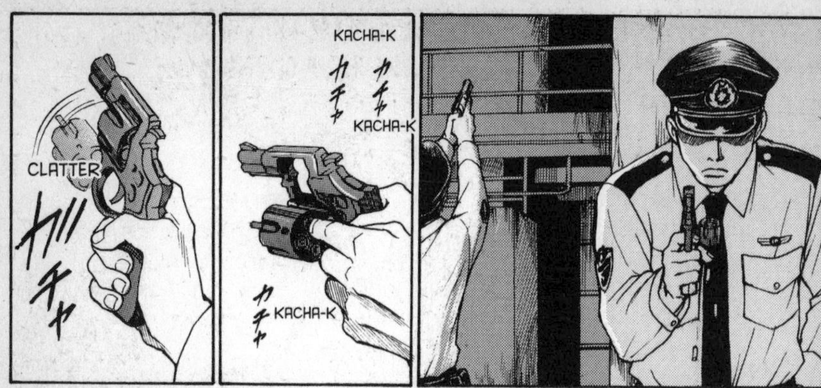

POW
POW
Just how many bullets do they have?
This is like war.
Are they trying to relieve their daily frustration?
I can't stand it any longer. They might shoot us just to relieve their stress.
POW

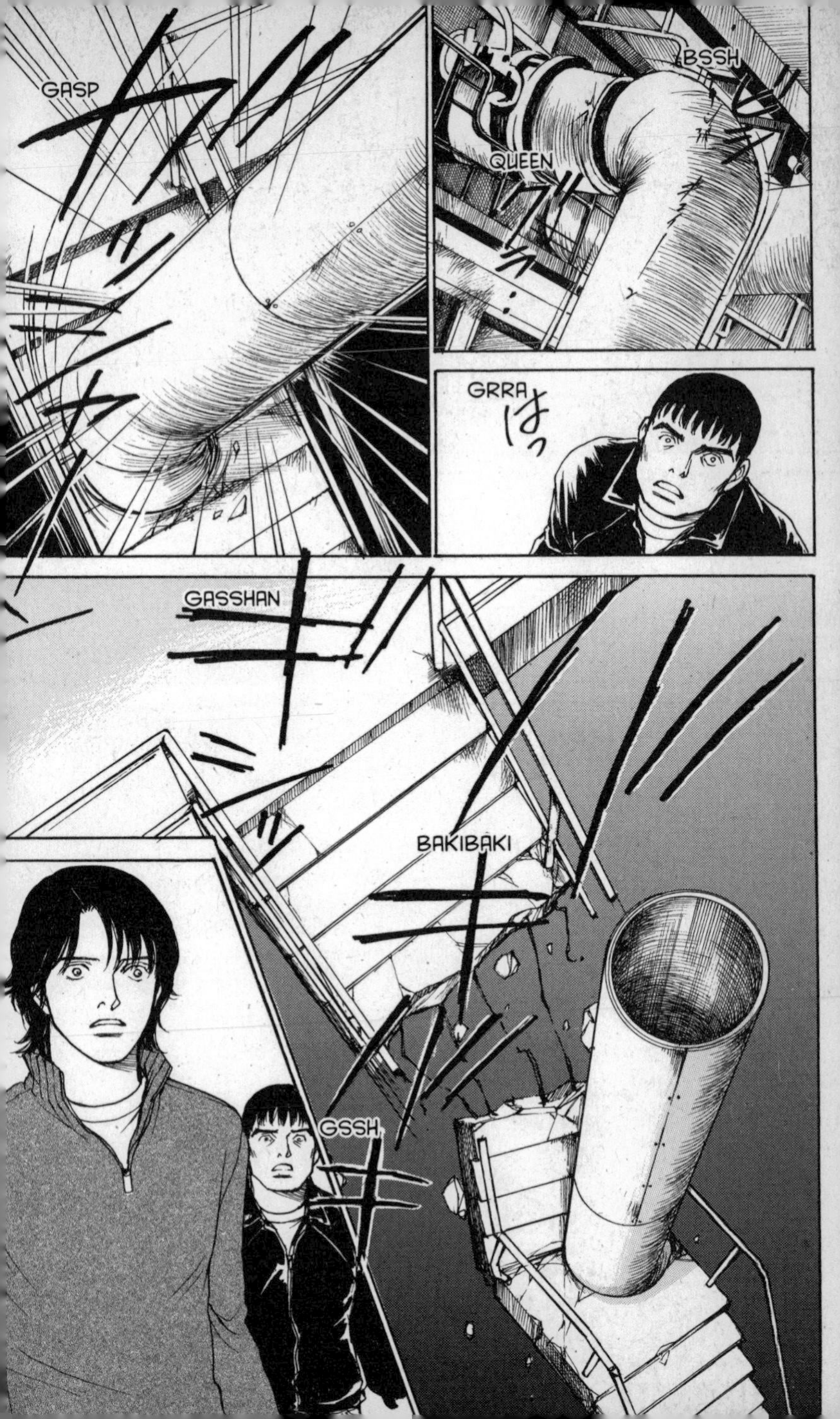
BSSH
QUEEN
GRRA
はっ
GASP
GASSHAN
BAKIBAKI
GSSH

Shoot
Now we can't use the stairs.
It's your fault for making them shoot all over the place.
You told me to make them do it.
You should have controlled them better.
Maybe you should deal with it by yourself.

Wa...wait a minute, are you just going to leave me here?
Who cares. It's not like I wanted to be here in the first place.
Don't say that. We're friends, aren't we?
What do you mean, we're friends!?

BEEP
ファン
BEEP
ファン
!
Shoot, more cops. If we don't leave now, we're finished.
But how are we going to get out?
Cool! Behind the building is a river. If we jump off from here, we may be able to escape.
You're kidding. The water is dis-gusting.
This is no time to be picky.
GASSHAAN

This reminds me of the old days.

First it was fire, now it's sewer water.

This isn't going to be pretty.

SPLASH

SPLASH

BEEP
ファン
BEEP
ファン
BEEP
ファン
BATAN
バタン
BATAN
バタン
This is the police. We have you surrounded.
Drop your weapons and step outside!

Wasn't that fun?

I'll show you something exciting again soon.
The next one will be even better.

The end of #16 Escape

URO URO

#17 THE LIGHT

I'll go check on Sakaki-san. You stay home.
Wait. I'm coming with you!

No way.
If you come, you'll just make more work for us, okay?

Remember who you're dealing with. Something terrible could happen to me, too.

It's Isaac I'm fighting. I may be the one to lose this battle.

GASP
DING DONG

BAM
BAM
Kujyou-san, it's me, Sakaki! Please open the door.
Sakaki-san?
I'm with Shuro. Open up.
TMP
TMP
TMP
GACHA-K
I'm glad you guys are safe.
402
KUJYOU

GOWN
GOWN
UWAH.
This stinks!
Even in an emergency, I'm amazed you guys dived into raw sewage.
Well, I guess it is better than getting shot.
SIGH
I'm glad I didn't go with you guys.

We offer our apologies for today's disaster.
The police department has yet to explain this afternoon's shooting incident involving several police officers.
This has only added to widespread public distrust of the police force.
A total of thirteen police officers participated in the shooting. Two officers were shot in the stomach and are in critical condition. Five officers suffered leg and arm injuries.
I guess they all survived.

To you, I'm nothing more than a guinea pig.
...
It's so weird that you're thanking me.
Thanks to you.
In fact, I have you to thank for all of this.
For you scientists—
Am I wrong?
Do you really believe that's how we perceive you?
What makes me different from your other guinea pigs?
Until very recently, I'd never seen the outside world.
I was just a thing born in a test tube and raised in the lab.

I guess you're right.

Now that I look back, I can see how selfish and cruel we were.
In my mania to create life, I somehow became the kind of person who's all too willing to take it.

And here I am trying to kill Isaac, for my own selfish reasons.
You must feel like Isaac is our own twin. You must be so angry with ne for trying to kill him.

Isaac
must
die.

!

Now that I've seen him again I know he's only gotten worse since leaving the lab.

He enjoys killing people?

He's proud of his powers.

He destroyed the lab to save his own life. But this time, he was truly enjoying himself..

...by killing other people.

Before he learned right from wrong, he knew he had power over life and death.

Now that he's out in the world, he knows just how powerful he is.

Do you under-stand how he feels?
Of course. We belong to the same species.

Don't worry. I'm not aggressive like him.
We were both just guinea pigs. But we had different upbringings, so we've grown apart.
For good or ill, I was always treated well, like a pet, but he was treated like something disposable.
Without realizing it, you've created a totally destructive force.

And now the dark side of modern society has warped his mind.
One day, Isaac will be a threat even to me. I can't let him survive.

Th... then...

I'll help you out...

...as much as I can.

Oh, no, you ripped my robe.
It was a gift from the wife of the head of the science lab I worked at in America.
I'm not used to wearing women's clothes. Don't you have any men's clothing here?
Of course not. I'm a single woman.
Ah... well... um...
But you must have been with men? Don't you have a jacket or something?
Eh...?
You don't have any...
You've been with a man before, right?
TURN
くるっ
BATA-M
バタン
......

That's not the right way to talk to a woman.

Has she really been single for more than twenty years?

The guys at the university lab say she's failed at omiai a total of twelve times.

I'm staying at my girlfriend Kimiko's place. Sakaki-san, you may stay here.
I'll leave some cash so you can get some food.

Ah...Don't worry about me. Once my clothes are dry, I'll get out of here.

No, don't. You're wanted by the police because of the shooting incident.

The boy who was Isaac's substitute saw your face. It's too dangerous for you to be running around outside.

If you really thin you need ne clothes, g to the conv nience stor and get son shirts and underwear.
But otherwise, I think you should avoid leaving the apartment.

And here you go!

What is this?

A sewing set.
By the time I get back, I expect my robe to be fixed.

CHUCKL

......

CHUCKLE
クスッ

What's so funny?

I'm just picturing Sakaki-san sewing.
You're right.
It would be funny. We should have set up a video camera and caught it on tape.

Thank you for every-thing today.

You saved Sakaki-san's life.

And you've agreed to help us.

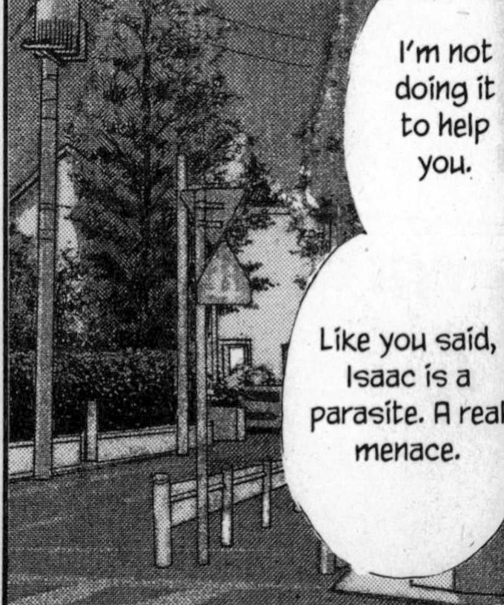

I'm not doing it to help you.
Like you said, Isaac is a parasite. A real menace.

Anyway, let's hurry up and get to your friend's house.
We'll miss the last train.

Thank you for taking me home.
Well, we were headed in the same direction.
And this is how a man should treat a lady, right?

What do you mean?
The guys at school told me hat this is what men do.

CHUCKLE

CHUCKLE
クスッ
Sure, but in ou case the purpose i a little different.
Usually, it's a gesture to show your interest in someone you have a crush on.
You didn't research that thor-oughly.

Next time, choose the right lady to impress.

She really is slow.

Oh?
What do you mean I'm slow?
No... never mind.

—The end of *ES*, Vol. 2 —

Translation Notes

Japanese is a tricky language for most Westerners, and translation is often more an art than a science. For your edification and reading pleasure, here are notes on some of the places where we could have gone in a different direction in our translation, or where a Japanese cultural refer-ence is used.

Japanese funeral, page 72

At Japanese funerals, a photograph of the deceased is displayed in the middle of a special Buddhist altar in the family home and surrounded by six lanterns. It is believed that the spirit of the deceased rests in this alta

Burning incense for the soul of the deceased, page 108

It is usual, as part of Buddhist funeral rituals, for friends and relatives of the deceased to visit the bereaved family. Visitors burn incense at the altar (described above) while praying for the departed soul to rest in peace.

uddhist altar, page 109

ter a person's death, the family elects and displays a Buddhist tar, usually made of gilded or nusual foreign wood. At right, ou can see the photo displayed n the altar, along with the incense fering and a metal prayer bowl, hich visitors ring with a special ick, shown in the lower right of e panel. The box with the ribbon olds Kojima-san's ashes.

miai, page 218

Has she really been single for more than twenty years?
The guys at the univesity lab say she's failed at omiai a total of twelve times.

miai is a matchmaking system for dividuals seeking a serious relationship ith the prospect of marriage. In this system, an individual asks friends, parents, latives, a professional matchmaker, or ven their boss to set them up with rmal dates.

The term *omiai* is used to describe both the entire process and the first eeting. The first meeting is often carried out in an expensive tea shop hotel with all present dressed in formal attire. The couple's parents nd the matchmaker are usually in attendance, too, though they seldom tend any later meetings. Either side may freely terminate the *omiai* at ny time. If one party declines another meeting or date after a few formal eetings, the message is usually communicated through the matchaker. Traditionally, the couple decided to marry after having several ates, and *omiai* was used primarily to find a marriage partner. Nowaays, it is more common for men and women to date extensively after the *miai* before choosing to marry, so the *omiai* is really now used as a way finding compatible dates, especially by busy or shy people.

Preview of *ƐS*, Vol. 3

We are pleased to present you with a preview of Vol. 3. This volume will be available in English soon. For now you'll have to make do with the Japanese!

秋庭くん!?

BY OH!GREAT

Itsuki Minami needs no introduction—everybody's heard of the "Babyface" of the Eastside. He's the strongest kid at Higashi Junior High School, easy on the eyes but dangerously tough when he needs to be. Plus, Itsuki lives with the mysterious and sexy Noyamano sisters. Life's never dull, but it becomes downright dangerous when Itsuki leads his school to victory over vindictive Westside punks with gangster connections. Now he stands to lose his school, his friends, and everything he cares about. But in his darkest hour, the Noyamano girls give him an amazing gift, one that just might help him save his school: a pair of Air Trecks. These high-tech skates are more than just supercool. They'll enable Itsuki to execute the wildest, most aggressive moves ever seen—and introduce him to a thrilling and terrifying new world.

Ages: 16 +

Special extras in each volume! Read them all!

VISIT WWW.DELREYMANGA.COM TO:

- Read sample pages
- View release date calendars for upcoming volumes
- Sign up for Del Rey's free manga e-newsletter
- Find out the latest about new Del Rey Manga series

Air Gear © 2003 Oh!great / KODANSHA LTD. All rights reserved.

KURO GANE

BY KEI TOUME

AN EERIE, HAUNTING SAMURAI ADVENTURE

Teen: Ages 13+

Avenging his father's murder is a matter of honor for the young samurai Jintetsu. But it turns out that the killer is a corrupt government official—and now the powers that be are determined to hunt Jintetsu down. There's only one problem: Jintetsu is already dead.

Torn to pieces by a pack of dogs, Jintetsu's ravaged body has been found by Genkichi, outcast and master inventor. Genkichi gives the dead boy a new, indestructible steel body and a talking sword—just what he'll need to face down the gang that's terrorizing his hometown and the mobster who ordered his father's hit. But what about Otsuki, the beautiful girl he left behind? Steel armor is defense against any sword, but it can't save Jintetsu from the pain in his heart.

Special extras in each volume! Read them all!

VISIT WWW.DELREYMANGA.COM TO:

- Read sample pages
- View release date calendars for upcoming volumes
- Sign up for Del Rey's free manga e-newsletter
- Find out the latest about new Del Rey Manga series

Kurogane © 1996 Kei Toume / KODANSHA LTD. All rights reserved.

5 Graphic S
DETROIT PUBLIC LIBRARY
3 5674 04386475 1

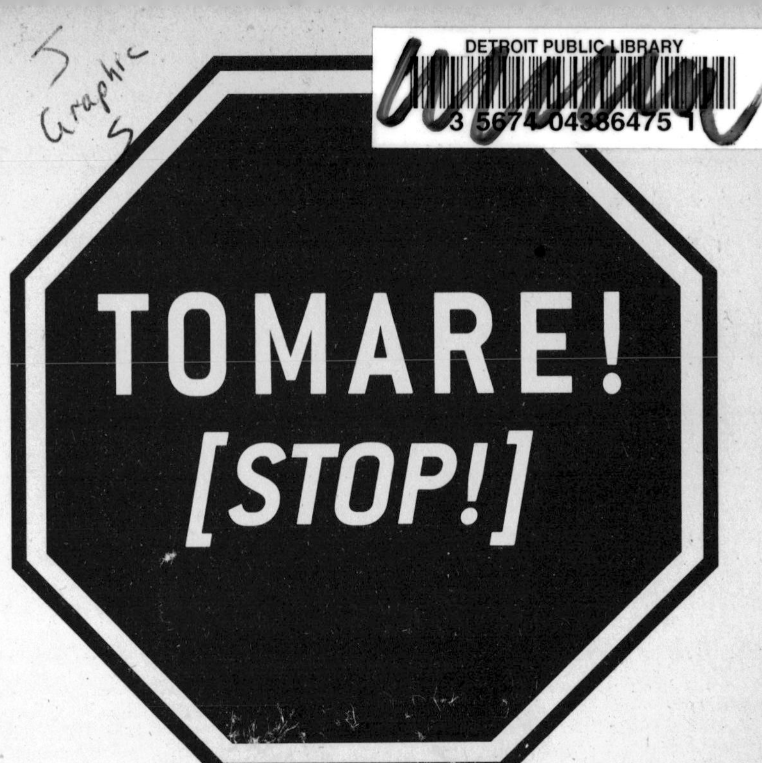

You are going the wrong way!

Manga is a completely different type of reading experience.

FRANKLIN BRANCH LIBRARY
13651 E. MCNICHOLS RD.
DETROIT, MI 48205
(313) 852-4797

To start at the beginning, go to the end!

That's right! Authentic manga is read the traditional Japanese way—from right to left. Exactly the opposite of how American books are read. It's easy to follow: Just go to the other end of the book, and read each page—and each panel—from right side to left side, starting at the top right. Now you're experiencing manga as it was meant to be.

DEC - - 2008 R